Sacraments Revisited

Sacraments Revisited

What Do They Mean Today?

LIAM KELLY

Foreword by
Vincent Nichols

Paulist Press
New York, Mahwah

Published by arrangement with
Darton, Longman and Todd Ltd
1 Spencer Court
140–142 Wandsworth High Street
London SW18 4JJ

Published in the USA by
Paulist Press
997 Macarthur Boulevard
Mahwah, NJ 07430

Reprinted 2001

ISBN: 0–8091–3812–3

Imprimatur	**+ The Rt Revd James J McGuinness**
	Bishop of Nottingham
Nottingham	**25 June 1997**

Designed by Sandie Boccacci
Phototypeset in 10/13pt Palatino by Intype London Ltd
Printed and bound in Great Britain by
Page Bros, Norwich

Contents

Acknowledgements

All biblical quotes are taken from *The Jerusalem Bible (Standard Edition)*, published and copyright 1966, 1967 and 1968 by Darton, Longman and Todd Ltd and Doubleday & Co Inc.

Quotes from the documents of the Second Vatican Council are taken from *Vatican Council II – Constitutions, Decrees, Declarations*, General Editor Austin Flannery, O.P., published jointly by Costello Publishing Company, Inc., New York and Dominican Publications, Dublin, 1996, by kind permission of Austin Flannery, O.P., Dominican Publications, Dublin.

Excerpts from the English translation of *Rite of Marriage* © 1969, International Committee on English in the Liturgy, Inc. (ICEL); excerpts from the English translation of *Rite of Baptism for Children* © 1969, ICEL; excerpts from the English translation of *Rite of Penance* © 1974, ICEL; excerpts from the English translation of *Rite of Confirmation*, Second Edition © 1975, ICEL; excerpts from the English translation of *Ordination of Deacons, Priests, and Bishops* © 1975, ICEL; excerpts from the English translation of *Pastoral Care of the Sick: Rites of Anointing and Viaticum* © 1982, ICEL; excerpts from the English translation of *Rite of Christian Initiation of Adults* © 1985, ICEL. All rights reserved.

Extract from *The Book of Sacramental Basics* by Tad Guzie, © Paulist Press, used with permission.

Extract from *Communicating Christ to the World* by Carlo Maria Martini, Sheed & Ward, 1994, reprinted with permission of Sheed & Ward, 115 E. Armour Blvd., Kansas City, MO 64141. 1.800.333.7373.

Extract from *The Concise Oxford Dictionary of the Christian Church*, edited by E. A. Livingstone, 1977, an Oxford University Press Publication, by permission of Oxford University Press.

Extracts from *Doors to the Sacred* by Joseph Martos, published by Triumph Books/Liguori Publications, and from *The Story of the Mass* by Pierre Loret, C.SS.R., published by Liguori Publications, used with permission.

Extract from *Focus on Faith* by Deborah M. Jones, © Copyright by Kevin Mayhew Ltd. Reproduced by permission from *Focus on Faith* by Deborah M. Jones.

Extracts from *Survival Guide to Confirmation* by Stephen Gomez, © St Pauls, Slough, 1993, reproduced with permission.

Extracts from the *Veritas Pre-Baptism Programme* © First published by *Veritas Publications*. Used with permission.

I am grateful for the assistance of Bishop Vincent Nichols. His encouragement and comments as the work was being put together have been invaluable.

Foreword

Actions, we are told, speak louder than words. Surely this is so because of the dichotomy which so often exists between what we say and intend on the one hand, and what we actually do, on the other.

With God no such dichotomy can exist. God's words and actions are in perfect harmony. There is no gap between what God says and what God does. Indeed, from all eternity the Word of God is the second person of the Trinity, fully God yet distinct from the Origin or Father of all. Indeed we can think of this second person, known as the Son because he takes flesh in Jesus of Nazareth, as God as known to God.

In Christ, who is God's word and God's action there is, then, no dichotomy, no gap at all between word and deed. His words and deeds take place not only in the life of Jesus, the Word made flesh, but also in his continuing active presence of Christ in the life of the Church.

It is particularly in the sacraments of the Church that the words and actions of Christ continue to be expressed without any dichotomy between them. In the sacraments words and actions correspond entirely, by virtue of the Holy Spirit, who brings to effect the word that is spoken and the action that is performed. As Father Herbert McCabe has said: 'In the sacraments God shows us what he does and does what he shows us.'[1*] In the sacraments, then, we come into full communication with the mystery of God for their words and actions not only disclose the activity of God in our world and in our lives, but they also bring about anew the full effectiveness of that activity.

This book gives a full account of the sacraments of the

*For Notes see pp. 169ff.

Church. It presents their origins in the words and actions of Christ and their development through the history of the Church. Furthermore, it does so in a manner which is accessible and inviting. This book will, therefore, be extremely helpful to catechists and those who make themselves available for the work of bringing others to the sacraments. It will help our current understanding of the sacraments, and our celebration of them, to be more firmly rooted in the developing tradition of the Church.

Sacraments are always an action of God, Father, Son and Holy Spirit, using the instrumentality of the Church. We celebrate them with joy and trust, knowing that in their words and actions we are being drawn into the very life of God, in whom we find our fulfilment and our salvation.

THE RT REVD VINCENT NICHOLS
16 June 1997

Introduction

Sacrament is a very religious word, and yet a well-known one. One of the things that is perhaps most commonly associated with religion and churches is the way they celebrate sacraments. And our memories, our experience of those celebrations will vary. You may have fond memories of a wedding, a baptism, First Holy Communion; you might have heard old stories (hopefully not true!) of a frightful moment known as 'First Confession'; or maybe you haven't experienced them, but are wondering what these special moments are, these special celebrations which seem so important to so many people? What are these special events that are at the heart of so many different Christian groups? This book is an attempt to reflect on those moments we call 'sacraments', to enquire about them and to re-visit them.

In seminary I remember lengthy courses on 'Sacramental Theology', with exams on the how and why of celebrating the sacraments. The aim, of course, was to give seminary students a basic understanding of the sacraments and a clear notion of how they are to be celebrated. This rightly added a pastoral dimension to what could easily become a purely academic exercise, ploughing through centuries of erudite scholarship. That phrase 'pastoral dimension' meant a lot more than, for example, remembering when a priest has to 'make' his Mass intention (the answer being, at least before the consecration, and to be valid the intention must be at least habitual, implicit, and absolute!).

For many adults, the notion of how important the sacraments are has been an integral part of religious up-bringing. This was perhaps expressed in phrases still heard today, especially with regard to the Mass, such as 'You mustn't miss Mass', or 'Where can I get Mass?'. Even if some of the expressions may have sounded negative, there lay behind them a deep love of faith and an implicit understanding of the fundamental importance of the sacraments. From childhood, in many Catholic families, what we needed to know about the seven sacraments was passed on with ever-increasing significance. Preparation for First Confession and First Communion were major events. And yet all I really remember about my First Communion is that I had to wear a red tie (with elastic string at the back to hide under your collar) and had a boiled egg and jelly and ice-cream at the 'First Communion Breakfast'.

As I look back on this religious up-bringing, a few basic points remain embedded in my mind. I remember how important it is to go to Mass and how important confession is (although I might often say the same sort of things every time I go to confession). And there is something lurking in the back of my mind about being a 'soldier for Christ', from confirmation classes.

It is, I think, fair to say that for many adults there is a danger that some of the ideas about sacraments that we were taught as children have never been taken any further. This is seen best of all in the way we approach the Sacrament of Reconciliation. For many of my teenage years it would seem that the only sins I committed were 'swearing, telling lies, and taking God's name in vain'. Yet I assure you I was no saint! How easy it was to get into the 'shopping-list' mentality and reel off a list of sins. Today, we may still be reciting the same 'list' of sins that we have been reciting for the last ten, twenty years. As I go around parishes working with parents whose children are being prepared for their first celebration of the Sacrament of Reconciliation, I can almost guarantee that the parents will not have heard that the Catholic Church published a 'new' *Rite of Penance* in 1973, approved for use in England and Wales in 1976. If the Sacrament of Reconciliation were to be taken as a yard-stick, then it would seem that a more 'adult' approach to the sacrament is much needed. Although it would be wrong to use the cliché 'familiarity breeds contempt', it would be true to say that habits, both good and not so good, can be formed through regular and sometimes 'automatic' celebration of the sacraments.

And so a notion of 're-visiting' the sacraments comes to mind. If we go on holiday somewhere and take lots of photographs, we may look at those photographs some months or years later. It is a reminder of the place we were, helping to re-kindle the emotions, re-live the experiences. What we experienced and learned about a place can be 're-visited'. We can even encourage others to visit the same place by telling them about the good time we had, showing them the photos, sharing our experiences with them. In time, they might become visitors.

So it can be with the sacraments. As adults, we may not have given the sacraments much thought since we first experienced them, since we first celebrated them. Or we might be interested in what happens, we might have friends who seem content to go to church every week, and would like to know a bit more.

This book, then, is an opportunity for us to 're-visit' the sacraments, to rediscover (or discover for the first time) the richness which lies within the celebration of them. For some people this may not be a new exercise, for others it may be a completely new experience. This book is not an attempt to force people to 'share', which can be uncomfortable, but an opportunity for us all to reflect. As adults, we might never have reflected on what the sacraments mean to us today. For those who are used to celebrating the sacraments, I believe there is a great temptation to stop thinking about them because we are 'grown-ups'. It is as if there is a check-list of sacraments, that we tick off as we receive each one (again, reflected in language which talks about children being 'done', or baptised). 'Grown-up' implies a process that comes to an end, or a stage we have arrived at: 'Wait 'till you're grown-up before you do that!'

Our faith should always be in a stage of 'growing-up'. Or, as one Jesuit professor said to me as I expressed my delight at the end of the university exam session, 'Liam, exams never come to an end!' It would be sad, then, if the way we approach the sacraments never changed, never developed, if we thought that we had 'made it' in terms of faith. Some people might say that sacraments today have lost their vitality, their unique air of mystery; that there is nothing to celebrate; that we don't have to go to church to pray to God; that sacraments are just social functions ('wetting' the baby's head, having a First Communion Party, and so on). Whatever our idea of sacraments may be, it is important to reflect on what they mean to us as individuals, and not take them for granted.

> Sacraments are 'powers that come forth' from the Body of Christ, which is ever-living and life-giving. They are actions of the Holy Spirit at work in his Body, the Church. They are 'the masterworks of God' in the new and everlasting covenant.[1]

This book is an opportunity to reflect on what these 'masterworks' mean today.

How This Book Might Be Used

To help us understand the seven sacraments of the Church, the first chapter provides a theological background to the whole idea of 'sacraments'. This is our first reflection, for which an historical and theological background is provided.

The subsequent chapters will deal with each of the sacraments individually, providing first an historical and theological background, and then an opportunity to examine how each sacrament can be a deeper part of our faith today.

The materials contained in this book are aimed at anybody who might wish to reflect on the meaning of sacraments today. Any reading and reflection can be done by individuals, in groups, or across parishes and denominations. For example, the celebration of a particular sacrament in a parish might provide an ideal opportunity for parents and/or catechists to reflect together on what the sacrament means to them. The reflections in this book can be adapted to suit your needs.

1 Sacraments – An Overview

'Sacrament' – word and definition

Jesus never used the word 'sacrament' and it is not found in the Bible. The word 'sacrament' translates the Latin word *sacramentum*. This was an oath, particularly a soldier's oath of allegiance to his leader or emperor and the Roman gods. The first word used for what we now call 'sacraments' was the Greek word for 'mystery', *mysterion*, a pagan word used to describe cults people were initiated into.

In his book *Waterhouse on Newspaper Style*, the journalist Keith Waterhouse tells the story of an economics expert writing for *The Times*. He was approached by a young sub-editor who could not understand his latest article, and the expert is supposed to have said: 'That piece is meant to be understood by only a dozen people, and you're not one of them.' Is 'sacrament', I wonder, one of those pieces of religious jargon understood by those in the know, but simply recognised as a piece of technical language by everybody else? Or is it a word many think they know the general meaning of without really being able to put their finger on a precise meaning?

Let us now turn to definitions, since although they do not provide all the answers, they can be useful in guiding our reflections along certain paths.

> 249. What is a Sacrament?
>
> A Sacrament is an outward sign of inward grace, ordained by Jesus Christ, by which grace is given to our souls.[1]
>
> (*A Catechism of Christian Doctrine*)

68. What is a sacrament?
A sacrament is a sacred sign by which we worship God, his love is revealed to us and his saving work accomplished in us. In the sacraments God shows us what he does and does what he shows us.[2]

(*The Teaching of the Catholic Church – A New Catechism of Christian Doctrine,* Herbert McCabe OP)

The sacraments of the New Testament were instituted by Christ the Lord and entrusted to the Church. As actions of Christ and of the Church, they are signs and means by which faith is expressed and strengthened, worship is offered to God and our sanctification is brought about. Thus they contribute in the most effective manner to establishing, strengthening and manifesting ecclesiastical communion. Accordingly, in the celebration of the sacraments both the sacred ministers and all the other members of Christ's faithful must show great reverence and due care.[3]

(*Code of Canon Law*)

The word *sacrament* for Catholics has now come to describe certain activities of the Church which express the presence of Christ acting in her.[4]

(*Focus on Faith,* Deborah M Jones)

A sacrament is a worldly reality which reveals the sacrament of salvation, because it is its realization.[5]

(*How To Understand the Sacraments* Philippe Béguerie – Claude Duchesneau)

The sacraments are efficacious signs of grace, instituted by Christ and entrusted to the Church, by which divine life is dispensed to us. The visible rites by which the sacraments are celebrated signify and make present the graces proper to each sacrament. They bear fruit in those who receive them with the required dispositions.[6]

(*Catechism of the Catholic Church*)

Some of these definitions will be more helpful than others. What unites them all is their attempt to put into words a living reality in the Church, to put down on paper what can be a rich faith-experience: receiving the sacraments.

REFLECTION

- A number of definitions of 'sacrament' have been provided. Are there any common threads linking the definitions? What words and images did you find useful?
- Think of any recent celebration of the sacraments which you may have attended or taken part in. Did the celebration relate to any of the definitions? If so, in what ways? If not, why do you think this was so?
- What does the word 'mystery' mean to you? Would you associate it in any way with sacraments?

Sacraments – the ideas develop

If Jesus didn't say it and the word 'mystery' doesn't adequately translate it, then where did the Church's understanding of sacraments come from? As will become clear, the Church had lived and experienced sacraments before defining them. Definitions are simply reflections on lived experience. What, then, was that experience?

The New Testament tells us something about certainly two of the sacraments, baptism and Eucharist. Indeed, these were key elements of the early Christian communities.

Baptism by water has great religious significance in the ministries of John the Baptist and of Jesus himself. 'And so it was that John the Baptist appeared in the wilderness, proclaiming a baptism of repentance for the forgiveness of sins' (Mark 1:4). Jesus himself is baptised (Mark 1:9–11) and at the end of his earthly ministry calls on the eleven to 'make disciples of all the nations; baptise them in the name of the Father and of the Son and of the Holy Spirit' (Matt. 28:19).

The dramatic events of Pentecost are related at the start of the Acts of the Apostles. Filled with the Holy Spirit, Peter stood up with the eleven and addressed the crowd:

> 'You must repent, and every one of you must be baptised in the name of Jesus Christ for the forgiveness of your sins; and you will receive the gift of the Holy Spirit.' . . . They accepted what he said and were baptised. That very day about three thousand were added to their number. These remained faithful to the teaching of the apostles, to the brotherhood, to the breaking of bread and to the prayers. (Acts 2:38, 41–42).

So here we have evidence of a ritual of baptism, as a sign of 'belonging to Christ and the community'. The communal meal – the Eucharist – is described as the 'breaking of bread' (see also Acts 2:46, 20:7).

The oldest account of what we today call the 'Mass' or 'Eucharist' occurs in Paul's first letter to the Corinthians, where he refers to the 'Lord's Supper' (1 Cor. 11:20):

> For this is what I received from the Lord, and in turn passed on to you: that on the same night that he was betrayed, the Lord Jesus took some bread, and thanked God for it and broke it, and he said, 'This is my body, which is for you; do this as a memorial of me'. In the same way he took the cup after supper, and said, 'This cup is the new covenant in my blood. Whenever you drink it, do this as a memorial of me.' (1 Cor. 11:23–5).

The gospels also provide their accounts of the Lord's Supper: Mark 14:22–6, Matthew 26:26–30, Luke 22:14–23. (Chapter 13 of John's gospel describes Jesus' action of washing his disciples' feet at the Passover meal with them. There is no account of the institution of the Eucharist.)

The early Christian community clearly celebrated certain rituals which were the mainstay of its life: baptism and Eucharist. What is important for us to note here is that these celebrations were known by their names and not by the term 'sacrament'. Such a generic term had not yet come into existence. We can perhaps say that the early Christian community was more concerned with recounting the experience than using specific terminology and providing precise definitions.

With no all-embracing vocabulary for sacraments in the early Church authors continued to describe the rituals of baptism and the Eucharist. For example, the *Apostolic Tradition* written by Hippolytus, probably a Syrian priest, in *c.* 215–17 contains a baptismal liturgy. Baptism is administered with a threefold profession of faith, accompanied by a threefold immersion. But once again, the word 'sacrament' is not used, although what happens is described in some detail.

Gradually, circumstances changed. Authors began to reflect on more than just what happened during a particular ritual, and one of the first terms that came into use was the Greek word *mysterion*. In the pagan world this word, simply translated as 'mystery', referred to rites of initiation guaranteeing salvation. It was taken up by Eusebius (*c.* 267 to *c.* 340), Bishop of Caesaraea. He called baptism a *mysterion*. Before Eusebius, however, we find one author who does use the Latin term *sacramentum*. Tertullian (*c.* 160 to *c.* 225) came from Carthage in North Africa and wrote a large number of theological works. In order to avoid confusion with any idea of pagan mysteries, he preferred the word *sacramentum* for many aspects of the Christian faith, including baptism and Eucharist.

> Looking for an equivalent of the Greek word *mysterion* for his Latin-speaking audience, he adopted *sacramentum* perhaps because it already referred to Roman religious rites – and he even accused the Greek mysteries of imitating the Christian sacraments! In a discussion on the meaning of baptism, Tertullian explained that it was similar to the *sacramentum* which was administered to Roman recruits when they entered the army. The *sacramentum* was a religious initiation; so was baptism. It marked the beginning of a new way of life; so did baptism. It was an oath of allegiance to the emperor; baptism was a promise of fidelity to Christ.[7]

And so for the first time we can see the origins of the word 'sacrament'. Because of Tertullian's writings *sacramentum* became a general term for the rite of Christian initiation, with great emphasis on the allegiance to Christ and the community implied therein. Of course, this does not mean to say that early Christian communities now had a rich, complete sacramental theology at their finger-tips. *Sacramentum* was a word now applied to many things as well as to the rite of Christian initiation. But the seeds of sacramental reflection had been sown.

REFLECTION

- Tertullian's comparison of baptism to the initiation of a Roman soldier examined the elements of initiation, new way of life and allegiance. Do you think this a useful way of looking at sacraments today? Are there any other comparisons you might make or elements you might include?
- Think about the roles played by the different characters who might be present at the initiation of a new recruit into the Roman legions. What similarities and differences can you see between that and Christian initiation?

St Augustine

The seeds had been sown by Tertullian – more detailed reflection on the sacraments (perhaps one of the earliest examples of 'sacramental theology') was to come with St Augustine (354–430). He was born in North Africa, and migrated first to Rome and then to Milan. Here he came under the influence of Ambrose, Bishop of Milan. Augustine became a Christian in 387 and returned to Africa, where he became Bishop of Hippo in 396. As one of the most influential writers in the history of the Church Augustine is not to be overlooked, and his development of sacramental theology has played a key part in the Church's view of sacraments.

In looking at the sacraments, and in particular the sacrament of baptism, Augustine came up against the views of a group known as the Donatists, who controlled many of the churches in north Africa. This group was named after their founder, Donatus, who was a bishop in Carthage.

At the start of the fourth century, when Christian persecution was at its height, many people had renounced their faith, including a number of the clergy (those who deserted their faith were 'apostates'). It was widely believed that these clergy had thereby lost their authority to function as clerics, even though some of them continued to baptise. After the end of the persecution, the question was raised as to whether those baptised by these clerics needed to be baptised again, by clerics who had not renounced their faith. The Council of Arles (314) decreed that these people need not be baptised again.

The Donatists disagreed. They believed that the Holy Spirit did not act outside the one, true, holy, catholic Church and that therefore the clerics who had renounced their faith had cut themselves off from the Church. The baptisms they performed, since they were done without the assistance of the Holy Spirit, were null and void.

It was Augustine who, in trying to resolve this problem, set down in writing some of the key assumptions held today concerning sacraments. The general practice of the Church at the time was *not* to re-baptise sinners and apostates; therefore, Augustine argued, there must be something permanent about baptism; and the Council of Arles had declared there was no need to re-baptise those originally baptised by an apostate; therefore, there must be something about the sacrament which does not depend on the minister performing it. And yet, even after baptism people committed sins; so there was something about the sacrament which was not out of the hands of the baptised and the minister.

Augustine concluded there were two effects of baptism, one which was permanent and one which could be lost by sin. This first was the 'seal' of baptism, the second was God's grace.

Here, for the first time, a distinction had been made between a sacramental rite and its benefits, and it was clear that these latter did not depend on the minister. In the centuries to come this idea would become central to the sacraments. Augustine had also referred to the sacramental 'seal', a character conferred by the sacrament. Again, in later years this idea would be extended to other rituals only performed once – confirmation and ordination.

Augustine's position in the development of sacramental theology is central to our understanding of sacraments. Although his comments were reserved largely for baptism and the Eucharist, his writings have a much broader influence. He also called a sacrament a 'visible sign of invisible grace'. In his *Letters* he referred to a *sacramentum* as a *sacrum signum*, a 'sign of a sacred thing.'[8] To refer this back to the debate on baptism, Augustine was saying that the rite of baptism was a sacrament because it was a sign of joining the Christian community, and the sacramental seal was a sacrament because it was a sign of being united with Christ.

It would be fair to say that Augustine goes on to call many things 'sacraments', since so many things were 'signs of sacred things'. In fact, almost anything in the world could be a sacrament. But what is essential here is that for the first time *sacramentum* can be seen as an accepted term for a particular rite, and that the term is also linked to its sign character. With Augustine we can see the beginning of an idea that sacraments are signs, pointing to and making present divine realities.

The 'sacramental seal'

Let us go back for a moment to take a more detailed look at an important idea reflected in Augustine's writings: the 'sacramental seal'. In more recent terms this has been referred to as the 'sacramental character', an indelible quality which some of the sacraments (baptism, confirmation, and ordination) imprint upon the soul.

Early developments of ideas concerning this 'seal' or 'character' arose precisely from the sort of problem we saw earlier, when questions came up about repeating certain sacraments. These problems were answered by turning to the Scriptures, where, especially in the New Testament, there are many examples of things belonging to God bearing his seal: 'I saw that in the right hand of the One sitting on the throne there was a scroll that had writing on back and front and was sealed with seven seals' (Rev. 5:1); 'Do not work for food that cannot last, but work for food that endures to eternal life, the kind of food the Son of Man is offering you, for on him the Father, God himself, has set his seal' (John 6:27); '[it is God] marking us with his seal and giving us the pledge, the Spirit, that we carry in our hearts' (2 Cor. 1:22). There was a distinct feeling among Christians that this was not simply a metaphor, but a reality. In some way Christians 'bore' the image of God, they were marked out differently. Once again, the expression of this was found in the Scriptures as it was held that many of the passages referring to an anointing with the Spirit were in fact another way of talking about being sealed with the Spirit. For example:

> But you have been anointed by the Holy One, and have all received the knowledge . . . But you have not lost the anointing that he gave you, and you do not need anyone to teach you; the anointing he gave teaches you everything; you are anointed with truth, not with a lie, and as it has taught you, so you must stay in him. (1 John 2:20, 27)

And of course, there is the striking text from the Acts of the Apostles: 'Now raised to the heights by God's right hand, he has received from the Father the Holy Spirit, who was promised, and what you see and hear is the outpouring of that Spirit' (Acts 2:33).

Clearly, then, there was a well-held view that some sacraments, by the outpouring of the Spirit, conferred a special image and likeness of God: set people apart. This was the seal, or character, imprinted on one's soul.

Further developments

It is worth noting that up to now the early Christian writers have reflected on baptism and Eucharist, rather than on a general 'sacramental theology'. They were reflecting on their experience, on how church practice shaped their lives. And it was that practice that was gradually sharpening reflections and would eventually lead to definitions. Other 'sacraments' had not been totally ignored, and their development will be seen in the individual chapters later in this book. Suffice to say the link between certain religious practices or rituals and a notion of 'sacrament' was not yet fully developed.

From the time of the fifth century, there were many developments in the life of the Church. Some rituals became more complicated, some were simplified, some new ones arose (as, for example, with the division of baptism and confirmation into two rituals). Gradually, seven major rituals seemed to be in place: the baptism of infants and converts, confirmation by the bishop, a rite of penance and forgiveness, the anointing of the dying, ordination of priests, marriage, and the Eucharist.

Reflection on these and other rituals became very popular among experts, as they tried once again to define 'sacraments'. St Peter Damien (1007–72) believed sacraments to be concrete signs of a holy thing, thereby opening up the definition of 'sacrament' to a very broad spectrum; lists of sacraments ranged from twelve upwards. Hugh of St Victor (d. 1142), a French Augustinian monk, returned to Augustine's definition of sacrament as a sign of something sacred, but found it too broad. He proposed that the sign needed to be of divine institution to be a sacrament. Another important step had been taken.

It was Peter Lombard (*c.* 1100–60), a teacher at the Cathedral School in Paris, who came up with a working definition of sacrament in his book of *Sentences* written in 1150. He wrote: 'Something is properly called a sacrament because it is a sign of God's grace, and is such an image of invisible grace that it bears its likeness and exists as its cause.'[9] He also spoke of the institution and efficacy of the sacraments, coming to the conclusion that there can only be seven sacraments: baptism, confirmation, penance, Eucharist, marriage, extreme unction, and ordination. He distinguished these from what have come to be called 'sacramentals' (such as holy water, statues, prayers, religious objects) because these latter are signs not causes of grace. A sacrament must be both.

Peter Lombard's list gradually became accepted as definitive, and in 1215 the Fourth Lateran Council named the seven sacraments in the first official list provided by a Council of the Church.

St Thomas Aquinas

The 'Doctor Angelicus', the Dominican Thomas Aquinas (*c.* 1225–74), did not add too much in terms of sacramental theology, but he gathered together many of the thoughts that up to now had been expressed by different theologians. His writings still influence the thought of the Church today, and so it is only right that our next stop on this historical journey through the sacraments should be with him. Much of his work had been enlightened by Aristotle, the Greek philosopher writing three hundred years before the Christian era. Many of Aristotle's works had been rediscovered and translated in the twelfth and thirteenth centuries, at the time Thomas Aquinas was writing his great theological work, the *Summa Theologica*.

According to Aristotle everything in the world is composed of 'matter' and 'form'. 'Matter' is what something is made of, what we can see, hear, touch, etc.; 'form' is the unchanging nature, what is intelligible about something, defining its matter. Thomas Aquinas and other theologians applied this distinction to sacraments, saying that sacraments, too, are made up of matter and form. In baptism, for example, the matter of the sacrament is water, while the form is the words used, the Trinitarian formula 'I baptise you, in the name of the Father, and of the Son, and of the Holy Spirit'. Here, then, we have the distinction between the concrete elements of a ritual and the meaning attached to it.

Aristotle's ideas, as applied by Aquinas, proved of great help in explaining one of the continual debates in the Church, the notion of bread and wine being changed into the body and blood of Christ. Some people argued that the presence of Christ in the Eucharist was simply a spiritual presence. To use some of the terms we have come across so far, something could not be sign *and* reality: either the bread and wine were signs of the body and blood of Christ, or they were the real thing.

Using Aristotle's terms, Thomas Aquinas explained that at the consecration the substance of bread and wine gives way to the substance of the body and blood of Christ (transubstantiation), while the accidents, or appearance, of bread and wine remain unchanged. This was caused by the words of consecration.

Sacraments, then, were made up of a number of elements. There was the *sacramentum tantum*, the sign itself. This was something concrete, like taking bread and wine and saying the words of consecration. This brought about the real presence of Christ in the Eucharist, the *res et sacramentum*, the sign and reality signified. What the sacrament ultimately aimed at, the reality alone, *res tantum*, was the grace of union with Christ. This was not a sign of anything else. Put another way, the final effect of the sacrament (*res*) is grace, and this is conferred through an intermediate effect (*res et sacramentum*).

Aquinas believed the term sacrament applied to a sign of some sacred reality. He argued that sacraments were necessary because we need signs. We live in a world where many things are expressed in signs: today, road signs convey important information, birthday cards express birthday wishes as a sign of love and affection, flowers are often given on Valentine's Day as a sign of love. Sacraments are one of the Church's signs, a sign of the presence of Christ.

These signs were God communicating with his people. And since it was God communicating, Aquinas and others believed that the effectiveness of the sacraments did not, therefore, depend on the minister. At the time of Aquinas this was quite a thorny theological problem, as Joseph Martos reveals in his work *Doors to the Sacred*:

> Early in the thirteenth century, theologians had wrestled with this question, and the main objections to saying that the sacramental effects did not depend at all on the minister or recipient came from those who envisioned cases where the rite might be performed in jest or in ignorance. Suppose, for example, that a child playfully poured water

over an unbaptized friend's head and said the words of baptism; would the friend be baptized? Or suppose that a priest were teaching a student how to say Mass and said the words of consecration over an unnoticed piece of bread; would it automatically become the body of Christ?[10]

It was rightly concluded that both the minister and the recipient of the sacrament must have the intention of participating, but the cause of the sacrament's effectiveness was the rite itself. From here derives the notion that a sacrament's effectiveness arises from 'the work worked', '*ex opere operato*'.

Christ communicates himself in the sacraments. With this idea, Aquinas believed the Eucharist to be the most important sacrament: 'The sacrament of the Eucharist is, in an absolute sense, the greatest of all the sacraments . . . in this sacrament Christ himself is present substantially. All the other sacraments are ordered to this one as to their end.'[11] The sacraments could also be compared to natural aspects of life, so that baptism would be linked with birth and the other sacraments would have similar links to life: maturity (confirmation), food (Eucharist), alienation (penance), human love (marriage), vocation (priesthood), and sickness and dying (extreme unction/anointing of the sick). In this way, it could be seen that through the sacraments Jesus was touching the most basic aspects of human life.

These are just some of the thoughts of Thomas Aquinas concerning the sacraments. His importance cannot be underestimated, for he gathered together the thoughts and experiences of twelve centuries of sacramental life. It may seem a very academic exercise, but it shows that the Church is continually reflecting on its lived experience.

REFLECTION

- St Augustine spoke about the 'seal' of the sacrament. What seal or character do you think is conferred by baptism, confirmation, and ordination?
- Sacraments have been described as 'signs'. Why do you think we need signs today? What 'signs' can you think of

in the Church which are not sacraments? How useful are they? Why aren't they sacraments?

- Transubstantiation was explained by Thomas Aquinas using terms from the Greek philosopher, Aristotle. Did you find his explanation useful, and how would you explain it today?
- Thomas Aquinas implied that there might be a hierarchical order to the sacraments. What do you think of this, and how would you portray your vision of sacraments?
- Given the idea of a hierarchical order of the sacraments, how would you fill in the boxes in the first diagram below and what comments would you make on the second?

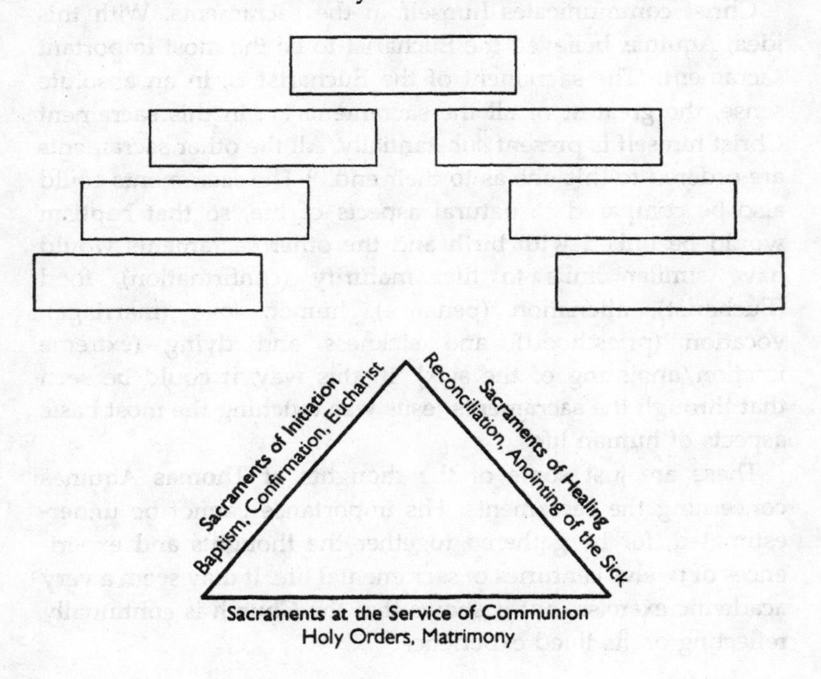

The Reformation

One of the more memorable events from school history lessons is the story of the Augustinian monk Martin Luther nailing his 'ninety-five theses' on the door of the cathedral in Wittenberg (Germany) in October 1517. On this document he listed his opposition to indulgences, part of the Catholic Church's sacramental system with regard to penance. In the early Church, sinners were required to perform harsh, public penances before returning to the community. Gradually these were lessened, as the Church became more lenient. By the time of the Middle Ages, popes were offering indulgences (remission of any punishment that might be due for sins) to those who took part in the Crusades. Later still, indulgences were offered in an attempt to encourage people to donate money to the Church. These abuses were challenged by Martin Luther. In 1520 Pope Leo X excommunicated him, condemning his writings in the Papal Bull *Exsurge Domine*. But the process of reform had begun and gathered pace in other parts of Europe.

It is beyond the task of this work to convey a complete picture of the Protestant Reformation and its far-reaching consequences. However, it is essential to grasp some basic principles which lay at the heart of this important movement.

At the outset, the reformers were unhappy with authority within the Church. It was not a question of what was to be believed, but how what was to be believed was decided. Rather than relying heavily on tradition, the reformers spoke of the individual's right to decide. They also turned to the authority of the Scriptures, as being more authentically religious than the authorities of the time. In simplistic terms, it might be said that while for both Catholics and reformers the ultimate authority was God, for the Catholics it was God speaking through the Church, while for the reformers it was God speaking through Scripture.

Abuses in many of the ways sacraments were celebrated in the Catholic Church led to a number of Protestant reformers adopting varying views of sacraments. Some continued to believe in seven sacraments, while at the other end of the scale some groups, known as Anabaptists, rejected even infant baptism and re-established the baptism of believers. Some believed in the divine effect of sacraments, some held that they had only social, human effects, while others held that sacraments had no effect at all.

In looking at Scripture, the main reformers tried to find evidence for the sacraments as instituted by Christ. A sacrament had to be a ceremony or sign instituted by Christ. For baptism and Eucharist, there was no problem (cf. Matt. 28:19 and 1 Cor. 11:23–5, and since these were ordained by Christ some dropped the name 'sacraments' and replaced it with 'divine ordinances'). The other sacraments had no scriptural basis for their institution by Christ and so the main reformers rejected them as sacraments and saw them simply as religious ceremonies.

The reformers' conclusions about these two divinely ordained rites varied. As regards baptism, Luther believed that salvation came through faith and not through works, and that this faith could be received by children and adults. The Anabaptists rejected baptism of children, believing that personal conversion must precede baptism. Calvin held that baptism was a sign of the grace that God continually offered to his people, and Ulrich Zwingli maintained that all sacraments presupposed faith.

As regards the Eucharist, similar differences arose. Luther believed in the real presence of Christ in the Eucharist, but used the term 'consubstantiation' (the presence of both real bread and wine, and the real body and blood of Christ). Ulrich Zwingli, however, saw Christ's presence to be merely symbolic, and the Eucharist was therefore a symbolic commemoration of the Last Supper. Calvin attempted to steer a path between the two.

In the eyes of the Protestant reformers the sacraments had been reduced to two. The Catholic Church now felt it had to respond.

The Council of Trent

Trent is a small town in northern Italy, not far from the Austrian border, with a population of under 100,000. In 1545 it became the site of the Catholic Church's response to Protestantism, when Pope Paul III called the world's bishops to a General Council that would last, with a number of interruptions, 19 years. The decrees issued by the Council of Trent were designed to reaffirm traditional Catholic teaching and to condemn any other views: *'anathema sit'*, 'those who hold such views are separated from the Catholic Church'. The Catholic counter-reformation had begun.

A sacrament was defined as 'a symbol of a sacred thing and

a visible form of invisible grace'.[12] For the first time in the history of the Church, it was defined as dogma ('a religious truth established by Divine Revelation and defined by the Church'[13]) that there are seven sacraments: 'If anyone says that the sacraments of the New Law were not all instituted by Jesus Christ our Lord; or that there are more or fewer than seven, that is: baptism, confirmation, the Eucharist, penance, extreme unction, Order and matrimony; or that any one of these is not truly and properly a sacrament, *anathema sit*.'[14]*

The bishops went on to say that the sacraments were necessary for salvation and conferred grace:

> If anyone says that the sacraments of the New Law are not necessary for salvation, but that they are superfluous; and that without the sacraments or the desire of them men obtain from God the grace of justification through faith alone, although it is true that not all the sacraments are necessary for each person, *anathema sit*.[15]

> If anyone says that the sacraments of the New Law do not contain the grace which they signify or that they do not confer that grace on those who do not place an obstacle in the way, as if they were only external signs of the grace or justice received through faith and a kind of mark of the Christian profession by which among men the faithful are distinguished from the unbelievers, *anathema sit*.[16]

The Council of Trent also confirmed the notion of *ex opere operato*, noting the importance for minister and recipient of the sacrament to have the right intention. Despite the rigid language of the Council's *Decree on the Sacraments*, this latter point reinforces the idea that the sacraments are not simply mechan-

* The phrase 'instituted by Christ' does not, of course, mean that he provided the words and gestures for every sacrament. It is stating that the sacraments derive their meaning and power from Jesus, and that all seven are consistent with the life, ministry and teachings of Jesus. The bishops at Trent wanted to define that sacraments are primarily gifts of God. Jesus *as God* instituted the sacraments. It is not part of defined faith that at a particular time, in a particular place, the historical Jesus instituted certain sacraments.

ical, or magical ceremonies. The role of the minister is important.*

From the Catholic Church's view-point, sacramental guidelines had been drawn up. In summary, the Council declared that the sacraments were instituted by Christ, that they are signs of sacred things, that there are seven sacraments, conferring grace, while three also confer an indelible character, and God's action does not depend on the minister. Protestant sacraments were invalid, with the exception of baptism (since this was performed in accordance with the New Testament understanding). The Council of Trent imposed a uniform view of the sacraments on the Catholic world, and for the next four centuries the uniformity of sacramental practice throughout the Catholic Church was to be interpreted as a sign of its spiritual unity. In some respects, the Council of Trent brought to a halt development in sacramental theology. It was if the Council had finally explained exactly what sacraments were; subsequent developments were to concentrate on the how of celebrating them with a standard sacramental practice throughout the Catholic world. In fact, only seven years after the end of the Council the *Roman Missal* was published, and this was to remain virtually unchanged until the time of the Second Vatican Council nearly four hundred years later.

REFLECTION

- The Council of Trent defined a sacrament as 'a symbol of a sacred thing'. How helpful is this definition and what does it mean to you?
- Sacraments 'confer grace on those who do not place an obstacle in the way'. What do you think the bishops were trying to say here, and how might it affect the way we receive the sacraments today?

* This point was to have important repercussions and parallels in ecumenical debates in modern times. At the time of the Council of Trent, a number of Catholic clergy had joined the Reformation and continued to celebrate the sacraments in their Protestant communities. The Council declared these sacraments were valid if those celebrating them maintained the Catholic understanding of the sacraments as they were celebrating them.

- 'If anyone says that in three sacraments, namely, baptism, confirmation, and Order, a character is not imprinted on the soul, that is, a kind of indelible spiritual sign by reason of which these sacraments cannot be repeated, *anathema sit*.'[17] What do you think this means?
- 'If anyone says that these sacraments are so equal to one another that one is not in any way of greater worth than another, *anathema sit*.'[18] The bishops at the Council of Trent are suggesting that baptism and Eucharist have greater rank and dignity than the other sacraments. Why do you think this is so?

Modern developments

In 1959, Pope John XXIII announced that he was calling an Ecumenical Council of the Church, with its main aim being *aggiornamento*, 'letting in the light of day'. The Second Vatican Council began in 1962 and ended in 1965. The Council gave an enormous impetus to changes of attitude in the Catholic Church concerning many different things, including relations with other Christians and other faiths, the relationship between the Church and the world, and the whole nature of the Church itself. As Pope John XXIII himself said at the opening of the first session of the Council: 'The substance of the ancient deposit of faith is one thing, the way in which it is presented is another.'

The Second Vatican Council should not be seen as a surprise venture sprung on an unsuspecting Church. Rather, it was part of a process of development that was sweeping through many areas of church life. This could be seen in things such as the Liturgical Movement, which in simple terms attempted to reflect on the origins of the Church's celebrations rather than simply an adherence to its rituals, and the renewed interest in biblical studies, initially in the Protestant Churches and then among a number of Catholic scholars.

In this era of development, the documents of the Second Vatican Council present the teachings of the Church with a clear, pastoral emphasis. The rigid, scholastic language of the Council of Trent was replaced by a vision which produced documents such as the *Pastoral Constitution on the Church in the Modern World*, the *Constitution on the Sacred Liturgy*, the *Dogmatic Constitution on Divine Revelation*, and the *Dogmatic Constitution on the Church*. Sixteen documents in all ushered in a new era for the Catholic Church.

But it was an era which was attempting to return to the roots of the Christian faith, and thereby shed the light of faith on modern times. This was certainly true in terms of sacramental theology, as made clear in the *Constitution on the Sacred Liturgy*, the first document to be published by the Council in December 1963: 'With the passage of time . . . certain features have crept into the rites of the sacraments and sacramentals which have made their nature and purpose less clear to the people of today. Hence some changes are necessary to adapt them to present-day needs.'[19] In practical terms, the immediate change was obvious: Mass was no longer in Latin. But it is clearly a disservice to the Council and to any idea we may have of sacraments to see change simply in those terms. Behind the Council documents was a whole vision of sacramental theology which opened new horizons for the Catholic Church.

Before looking at the Council's vision of sacraments, it is important to note one important development (although it is not within the scope of this work to examine it in detail): 'Christ when he was lifted up from the earth drew all humanity to himself. Rising from the dead he sent his life-giving Spirit upon his disciples and through him set up his body which is the Church as the universal sacrament of salvation.'[20] In a unique way the Church itself is described as a 'sacrament'. Applying some of the notions of 'sacrament' that we have seen up to now, the suggestion that the Church, too, is sacrament is clear: it is a sign, a symbol, of Jesus himself. The life and work of Jesus is expressed most clearly in the Church, the Body of Christ. The Church represents and fully makes present Jesus Christ, the Son of God. The Church is the visible presence of the invisible Christ. The Church, as 'universal sacrament of salvation', continues the work of Christ.

As regards the seven sacraments, their definition and role remained unchanged:

> The purpose of the sacraments is to sanctify people, to build up the body of Christ, and, finally, to worship God. Because they are signs they also belong in the realm of instruction. They not only presuppose faith, but by words and objects they also nourish, strengthen, and express it. That is why they are called sacraments of faith. They do, indeed, confer grace, but, in addition, the very act of celebrating them is most effective in making people ready to receive this grace to their profit, to worship God duly, and to practise charity. It is, therefore, of the greatest importance that the faithful should easily understand the symbolism of the sacraments and should eagerly frequent those sacraments which were instituted to nourish the Christian life.[21]

The role of faith is important here, and it receives further expression when this same document declares that the faithful should come to the sacraments 'with proper dispositions, that their minds be attuned to their voices, and that they cooperate with heavenly grace lest they receive it in vain'.[22]

Sacraments have a double aim: the sanctification of those who participate in them, and praise of God. It is interesting that the Council does not use the scholastic phrase *ex opere operato*. Although the notion is not rejected, it is replaced by the concept of Christ's presence and action in the sacraments:

> He is present in the Sacrifice of the Mass not only in the person of his minister . . . but especially in the eucharistic species. By his power he is present in the sacraments so that when anybody baptizes it is really Christ himself who baptizes. He is present in his word since it is he himself who speaks when the holy Scriptures are read in the Church. Lastly, he is present when the Church prays and sings, for he has promised 'where two or three are together in my name there I am in the midst of them' (Matt. 18:20).[23]

Christ, indeed, always associates the Church with himself in this great work in which God is perfectly glorified and men and women are sanctified. The Church is his beloved bride who calls to her Lord, and through him offers worship to the eternal Father.

The liturgy, then, is rightly seen as an exercise of the priestly office of Jesus Christ. It involves the presentation of humanity's sanctification in symbols 'perceptible by the senses and is carried out in ways appropriate to each of them. In it, complete and definitive public worship is performed by the mystical body of Jesus Christ, that is, by the Head and his members.'[24] Here, the emphasis is placed on the communal aspect of the sacraments, their public celebration. This receives its highest expression in comments on the Eucharist, when the Council declares it does not want people to be present at Mass 'as strangers or silent spectators'.[25] 'The rite of the Mass is to be revised in such a way . . . that devout and active participation by the faithful may be more easily achieved.'[26] There was a clear pastoral emphasis on the experiential nature of the sacraments, moving away from – but not rejecting – the traditional devout practices (such as the Rosary, Benediction, Stations of the Cross, etc.) which for some time had been a major aspect of some people's participation in the sacramental life of the Church.

The Second Vatican Council acknowledged the need to rethink the meaning of Christianity in the modern world, to read the 'signs of the times', and this is precisely what theologians did for the sacraments. The pastoral emphasis on the sacraments opened up new avenues, and in subsequent years experts have attempted to get behind the statements and concepts revealed by the work of the Council.

The Second Vatican Council did not make any specific mention of Jesus as sacrament, but such an understanding underpins much of its work. Jesus makes God present to us, and in this way is a sacrament of God. Through Jesus, we encounter the mystery of God.[27] Christ is the presence of God in the world. The humanity of Jesus is the visible reality, pointing to the divine reality itself. Jesus is the sacrament of all that God wishes to bestow on the world.

An unbroken sacramental line has been developed. The traditional seven sacraments can be traced to the Church, which is the sacrament of Christ, and to Christ himself, the sacrament of God. The sacraments are signs of both the Church and Christ, pointing to the action of Christ in the world, and communicating God's grace to that world.

One of the post-Vatican II emphases was very much on the experiential nature of the sacraments. They were seen as experiences that heightened awareness of what is sacred in human life. So the Eucharist, for example, would be seen in terms of a meal of special significance. This did not lessen or compromise any of the Church's teaching on the Eucharist, but rather offered an insight from experience. In this way, all the sacraments were seen as shedding new light on human experiences: the sacrament of marriage was linked to a call to fidelity, orders to service, reconciliation to conversion, confirmation to maturity. The sacraments also affirmed basic human needs: belonging (baptism), healing (anointing), and community (Eucharist).

The concept of community is important in sacramental theology. The sacraments are celebrated in public rituals and so they have a certain social significance. They are statements not just of an individual's belief, but a statement of what the community believes. As the Council said, they are 'sacraments of [the] faith' of the Church. Modern terminology often refers to sacraments as 'stages on the journey of faith'; in fact, they are stages on the journey of faith and life, for the two cannot be separated. We can see, then, that on the whole sacraments take place at important human stages of life: birth, maturity, cementing relationships, important decisions of adulthood, illness. In this sense, the sacraments affirm our humanity and consecrate it to God. Indeed, they can transform our human reality, for the sacraments are a call to 'put on Christ', to be Christ to others. So, for example, in the words of the Rite of Baptism: '*N.*, you have become a new creation, and have clothed yourself in Christ. See in this white garment the outward sign of your Christian dignity. With your family and friends to help you by word and example, bring that dignity unstained into the everlasting life of heaven.' Confirmation continues this process; reconciliation is not just about being forgiven, but is a call to be forgiving; at the table of the Lord we are fed by the Word of God and the Bread of Life, and sent out 'in peace to love and serve the Lord'; one of the Prayers After Anointing speaks of the transformation that God can bring to our human situation: 'When he/she is afraid, give him/her courage, when afflicted, give him/her patience, when dejected, afford him/

her hope, and when alone, assure him/her of the support of your holy people',[28] the sacrament of matrimony is 'so holy a mystery that it symbolises the marriage of Christ and his Church'; and finally, the sacrament of orders is one of service, transforming human nature into a ministry of service. The sacraments, then, are all invitations to a new way of life.

Since all these ideas are expressed in rituals, many of the latest ideas in sacramental theology come under the guise of liturgical theology. This has increased with the liturgical changes implemented by the Second Vatican Council. It is perhaps a direct result of the call for 'active participation', examining how that can be best achieved today. This is a new departure, for as we have seen the scholastic influence from Thomas Aquinas often presented sacraments as somewhat static events; hence the idea that sacraments were 'administered' and 'received', with a great emphasis on the validity of the sacrament. Indeed, in the Middle Ages great debates ensued concerning the legality of sacramental rites. A sacrament was licit if it was administered in accordance with all the regulations of the Code of Canon Law; to break any regulation rendered the sacrament illicit, or canonically illegal (although still sacramentally valid). Although our language today still speaks of 'receiving' the sacraments, the emphasis has shifted to examining the rituals themselves. Hence the tremendous volume of liturgical commentaries examining experience and meaning in the liturgy. These are an important resource for sacramental reflection today.

REFLECTION

- How do you see the Church as a sacrament? Can you think of ways at diocesan and parish level in which the Church is a sacrament in your area?
- The Second Vatican Council spoke of 'sacraments of faith'. What does this mean to you?
- How do you see Jesus as a 'sacrament' today?
- Sacraments can transform humanity, they are signs demanding a response. How do you respond to some of the

sacraments you may have recently celebrated or witnessed being celebrated?

- The experiential language used in relation to the sacraments (e.g. stages on the journey of faith) is a stark contrast to the metaphysical, scholastic language of Thomas Aquinas. Which analogies of sacraments do you find most useful, and why?

The Catechism of the Catholic Church

In 1985 the world's bishops asked for an authoritative compendium of the Church's teaching. The original request at the 1985 Synod of Bishops came from the bishops of Korea, Senegal and Mauritius and was expressed at the Synod by Cardinal Bernard Law, Archbishop of Boston in the United States. Nearly ten years later, on 29 May 1994, the English-language version of the *Catechism of the Catholic Church* was published. (The first edition, in French, was published in November 1992.)

Part Two of the *Catechism*, 'The Celebration of the Christian Mystery', sets out a contemporary understanding of the Church's sacraments. Following trends that we have just looked at, it examines sacraments through the liturgy, although this latter term has a very broad meaning: 'In Christian tradition it means the participation of the People of God in the "work of God". Through the liturgy Christ, our redeemer and high priest, continues the work of our redemption in, with and through his Church.'[29] The *Catechism* underlines the link between sacraments and the saving death and resurrection of Jesus. Through the sacraments we are united to that event. Again the community aspect of the sacraments is stressed, and the *Catechism* looks at five dimensions of sacraments today:

1. They are sacraments of Christ: 'The mysteries of Christ's life are the foundations of what he would henceforth dispense in the sacraments, through the ministers of his Church, for "what was visible in our Saviour has passed over into his mysteries".'[30]
2. They are sacraments of the Church, for they reveal the

essence of the Church and in them the Church 'acts . . . as "an organically structured priestly community".'[31]

3. They are sacraments of faith: 'The Church's faith precedes the faith of the believer who is invited to adhere to it. When the Church celebrates the sacraments, she confesses the faith received from the apostles – whence the ancient saying: *lex orandi, lex credendi* . . . The law of prayer is the law of faith.'[32] Faith is expressed and nourished through the sacraments.
4. They are sacraments of salvation: 'They are *efficacious* because in them Christ himself is at work.'[33] 'The Church affirms that for believers the sacraments of the New Covenant are *necessary for salvation*.'[34]
5. They are sacraments of eternal life, since through them the Church anticipates the end of time, 'when God will be "everything to everyone". . . . St Thomas sums up the various aspects of sacramental signs: "Therefore a sacrament is a sign that commemorates what precedes it – Christ's Passion; demonstrates what is accomplished in us through Christ's Passion – grace; and prefigures what the Passion pledges to us – future glory." '[35]

These ideas reflect recent shifts in sacramental understanding and the changing emphases that we have seen particularly from the time of the Second Vatican Council. The Council placed the Church firmly 'in and of the world', not aloof from it. And so the sacraments are seen as symbols of God's continued and active presence in that world, rather than means by which God breaks into a secular world. This also reflects the shift from seeing the saving effect of sacraments as solely a future reality to recognising their effect in the present. We are called to bring about God's kingdom now, to transform the world now, and so just as God's saving presence is not only something in the future, so the sacraments too can have an effect now. And the final shift is from seeing sacraments as purely individual, private events, between God and the recipient, to the community aspect of all sacraments, celebrated as public rituals. This is perhaps the most evident shift, seen, for example, as parishes opt for baptism to be celebrated during the Sunday community Mass, or as parishes have a communal Service of Reconciliation, and so on: 'It is the whole *community*, the Body of Christ united with its Head, that celebrates. "Liturgical services are not private functions but are celebrations of the Church which is 'the sacrament of unity'." '[36]

The *Catechism* was written to support the Church in its teaching role today. And one of the chief tasks in this sphere is that of liturgical catechesis, which 'aims to initiate people into the mystery of Christ . . . by proceeding from the visible to the invisible, from the sign to the thing signified, from the "sacraments" to the "mysteries".'[37] In the *Catechism*, the sacramental and liturgical worlds are fully merged.

REFLECTION

- Look at the following three groups of words and phrases. If you are happy to use the word/phrase because it is meaningful, draw a circle around it; if you use the word/phrase sometimes, but with caution, place a question mark next to it; if the word/phrase is dead for you and has little meaning, cross it out. Reflect on your answers and share them if you wish.

minister receive neglect make lapse encounter
administer celebrate

sacred action enactment sign action sacrament
expression of faith relationship mystery liturgical action
symbol liturgy action of the community

relational intimate communal efficacious simple
strengthening encouraging symbolic to build unity
nourishing incarnational receive neglect

- The following phrases about the sacramental life of the Church have been taken from a number of sources. Put a 'c' against those that leave you cold; an 's' against those you find useful; and an 'l' against those you find unclear and least helpful:

mystery of salvation
sacramental economy

sacramental economy
celebration of the mystery of Christ in worship, witness, service
powers of Christ
the rhythm that makes life human
privileged expressions of the covenant between Christ and the Church
actions of the Holy Spirit
sacred action surpassing all others
Sacraments manifest and communicate the mystery of communion with God
dull ritual that does not express anything meaningful
masterworks of God in a new and everlasting covenant
the heart of life
the dawning of the light for us
the Symbol of faith in which the Church confesses the mystery of the Trinity and the Paschal mystery

Try to compose your own definition of sacraments, or list the elements you would include in such a definition.

In talking about the sacraments, what sort of language do you find most helpful?

In what you have read so far is there anything that has struck you in any particular way?

Conclusion

Down the centuries, the way of looking at sacraments has changed and it will, I am sure, continue to change in the future. Vatican II brought a spirit of renewal, 'letting in the light of day', leading to new insights into the sacraments and the way we celebrate. Today, as we celebrate the sacraments with new Rites, we must continually re-visit them to renew the understanding we have gained from revelation, Scripture, the Church's teaching, history and our own experience. As we attempt to harmonise and reflect on all these things we must do so in a spirit of prayer, for let us remember that each sacrament is an activity accompanied by prayer.

To conclude this first section, and before we go on to look at the individual sacraments, I offer my own favourite definition of sacraments, taken from Tad Guzie's excellent work, *The Book of Sacramental Basics*:[38]

A sacrament
is a festive action
in which Christians assemble
to celebrate their lived experience
and to call to heart their common story.
The action is a symbol
of God's care for us in Christ.
Enacting the symbol
brings us closer to one another in the church
to the Lord
who is there for us.

2 *The Sacraments*

Jesus is a sign of God's love for us. Sacraments, too, are signs of God's love for us, offering us seven special ways to experience and respond to that love. Of course we should not look upon these seven sacraments as completely separate – there are unifying elements in the sacraments that we have already seen.

The *Catechism of the Catholic Church* provides a useful grouping of the seven sacraments which will guide us in our reflection:

> Christ instituted the sacraments of the new law. There are seven: Baptism, Confirmation (or Chrismation), the Eucharist, Penance, the Anointing of the Sick, Holy Orders and Matrimony. The seven sacraments touch all the stages and important moments of Christian life: they give birth and increase, healing and mission to the Christian's life of faith. There is thus a certain resemblance between the stages of natural life and the stages of spiritual life.[1]
>
> Following this analogy . . . the three sacraments of Christian initiation [will be treated first, followed by] . . . the sacraments of healing [and finally] . . . the sacraments at the service of communion and the mission of the faithful. This order, while not the only one possible, does allow one to see that the sacraments form an organic whole in which each particular sacrament has its own vital place. In this organic whole, the Eucharist occupies a unique place as the 'Sacrament of sacraments': 'all the other sacraments are ordered to it as to their end.'[2]

Sacraments of initiation

Baptism, confirmation, and Eucharist are considered the sacraments of initiation. St Thomas Aquinas viewed them in this way because through these sacraments one becomes a Christian. They are rites of entry, showing not just the importance of what is being undertaken but also offering a welcome from the community itself.

The *Catechism of the Catholic Church* sees these sacraments as a unit because they 'lay the foundations of every Christian life'.

> The faithful are born anew by Baptism, strengthened by the sacrament of Confirmation, and receive in the Eucharist the food of eternal life. By means of these sacraments of Christian initiation, they thus receive in increasing measure the treasures of the divine life and advance toward the perfection of charity.[3]

Sacraments of healing

Sacraments are a means of bringing wholeness, and two sacraments reflect the need for healing: the sacrament of penance or reconciliation restores the image of God within us that has been distorted by sin, while the sacrament of the anointing of the sick brings comfort in times of illness. These sacraments reveal Christ's power over sin and sickness:

> Through the sacraments of Christian initiation, man receives the new life of Christ. Now we carry this life 'in earthen vessels', and it remains 'hidden with Christ in God'. We are still in our 'earthly tent', subject to suffering, illness and death. This new life as a child of God can be weakened and even lost by sin.
>
> The Lord Jesus Christ, physician of our souls and bodies, who forgave the sins of the paralytic and restored him to bodily health, has willed that his Church continue, in the power of the Holy Spirit, his work of healing and salvation, even among her own members. This is the purpose of the two sacraments of healing: the sacrament of Penance and the sacrament of Anointing of the Sick.[4]

Sacraments of service to communion

For the final two sacraments – holy orders and matrimony – a new terminology is introduced: 'service to communion/to the community'. St Thomas Aquinas referred to these sacraments as being for the renewal of community and society.

> Baptism, Confirmation and Eucharist are sacraments of Christian initiation. They ground the common vocation of all Christ's disciples, a vocation to holiness and to the mission of evangelizing the world. They confer the graces needed for the life according to the Spirit during this life as pilgrims on the march towards the homeland.
>
> Two other sacraments, Holy Orders and Matrimony, are directed towards the salvation of others; if they contribute as well to personal salvation, it is through service to others that they do so. They confer a particular mission in the Church and serve to build up the People of God.
>
> Through these sacraments those already consecrated by Baptism and Confirmation for the common priesthood of all the faithful can receive particular consecrations. Those who receive the sacrament of Holy Orders are consecrated in Christ's name 'to feed the Church by the word and grace of God'. On their part, 'Christian spouses are fortified and, as it were, consecrated for the duties and dignity of their state by a special sacrament.'[5]

One of the important aspects of this new terminology is the emphasis on service and how even the personal holiness of those ordained or married stems from service of others. This should remove any false impressions the ordained or married might have about being 'holier than thou'.

The *Catechism*, then, has provided us with a useful grouping of the sacraments. It is by no means a perfect grouping and nor does it exclude any questions. However, for our purposes it provides a convenient structure for us to now go and re-visit the seven sacraments separately.

3 *Baptism*

Religion and statistics can sometimes be strange companions. They can lead to headlines such as 'Church proclaims "good news" as members return'[1] and 'Catholic Church loses Mass appeal'.[2] *The Daily Telegraph* article began: 'Parents eager to get their children into Church of England schools and the rise of evangelicalism [*sic*] have halted the long-term decline in Church membership, new statistics suggest.' The *Guardian* points out that despite the 'glamour of a string of celebrity converts such as the Duchess of Kent and Alan Clark, the Roman Catholic Church is losing its Mass appeal', with weekend Mass attendance for 1995 down 3 per cent on the previous year. And yet, in the Catholic Church, too, the numbers of Catholics are up, with about 75,000 children baptised every year. So it would seem that baptisms are up . . . while regular church attendance is at best 'bottoming out'. If this is the picture, what is the role of baptism?

Baptism and the early Church

Many people will be familiar with the figure of John the Baptist. He preached a 'baptism of repentance for the forgiveness of sins' (Mark 1:4), and even baptised Jesus himself. 'It was at this time that Jesus came from Nazareth of Galilee and was baptised in the Jordan by John. No sooner had he come up out of the water than he saw the heavens torn apart and the Spirit, like a dove, descending on him. And a voice came from heaven, "You are my Son, the Beloved; my favour rests on you".' (Mark 1:9–11). Clearly, baptism was an accepted ritual, and those baptised by John were expressing their change of heart, their conversion to his message. Jesus called on his apostles to 'go . . . and make disciples of all the nations; baptise them in the name of the Father and of the Son and of the Holy Spirit' (Matt. 28:19). According to the Acts of the Apostles, this is precisely what they did, beginning on Pentecost day itself after Peter's address to the crowds:

> Hearing this, they were cut to the heart and said to Peter and the apostles, 'What must we do, brothers?' 'You must repent,' Peter answered 'and every one of you must be baptised in the name of Jesus Christ for the forgiveness of your sins; and you will receive the gift of the Holy Spirit. The promise that was made is for you and your children, and for all those who are far away, for all those whom the Lord our God will call to himself'. He spoke to them for a long time using many arguments, and he urged them, 'Save yourselves from this perverse generation'. They were convinced by his arguments, and they accepted what he said and were baptised. That very day about three thousand were added to their number. (Acts 2:37–41)

This, and other episodes in the Acts of the Apostles (cf. Acts 8:26–34) suggest that the baptism conferred on such occasions was for adults who had expressed their faith in Jesus as the Christ (although there are some accounts of the baptism of entire households, as in the case of Lydia (Acts 16:11–15) and the gaoler at Philippi (Acts 16:25–33)). Adult baptism was the norm, and the ritual involved immersion in water (the Greek word *baptizein* means 'immerse'). It would appear that baptism was a new beginning, exemplified by the Pentecost account we have seen, as Peter called on the people to save themselves 'from this perverse generation'. Baptism brought about a real change in real lives.

The significance of this change was best expressed by a man whose conversion and baptism is perhaps one of the most dramatic stories in the early Church: Saul, who was to become known as Paul. ' "Brother Saul, I have been sent by the Lord Jesus who appeared to you on your way here so that you may recover your sight and be filled with the Holy Spirit." Immediately it was as though scales fell away from Saul's eyes and he could see again. So he was baptised there and then' (Acts 9:17–18). Paul, who had persecuted disciples of the Lord for some time, put behind him all that had been such an essential part of his life and joined a new community with a new way of life. This, Paul believed, was like the death and resurrection of Jesus. Immersion in water was dying to sin; coming out of the water was entering a new life with Christ:

> You have been taught that when we were baptised in Christ Jesus we were baptised into his death; in other words, when we were baptised we went into the tomb with him and joined him in death, so that as Christ was raised from the dead by the Father's glory, we too might live a new life.
>
> If in union with Christ we have imitated his death, we shall also imitate him in his resurrection. We must realise that our former selves have been crucified with him to destroy this sinful body and to free us from the slavery of sin. When a man dies, of course, he has finished with sin.
>
> But we believe that having died with Christ we shall return to life with him: Christ, as we know, having been raised from the dead will never die again. Death has no power over him any more. When he died, he died, once for all, to sin, so his life now is life with God; and in that way, you too must consider yourselves to be dead to sin but alive for God in Christ Jesus. (Rom 6:3–11)

The new way of life and new community resulting from baptism are expressed in many of Paul's other letters:

> You know perfectly well that people who do wrong will not inherit the kingdom of God: people of immoral lives, idolaters, adulterers, catamites, sodomites, thieves, usurers, drunkards, slanderers and swindlers will never inherit the kingdom of God. These are the sort of people some of you were once, but now you have been washed clean, and sanctified, and justified through the name of the Lord Jesus Christ and through the Spirit of our God. (1 Cor. 6:9–11)

> Just as a human body, though it is made up of many parts,

> is a single unit because all these parts, though many, make one body, so it is with Christ. In the one Spirit we were all baptised, Jews as well as Greeks, slaves as well as citizens, and one Spirit was given to us all to drink. (1 Cor 12:12–13)

Paul is careful, though, to point out that baptism is not some magic ritual that ensures automatic and eternal goodness on the part of the receiver. It was a call and a challenge to sin no more:

> From now onwards, therefore, we do not judge anyone by the standards of the flesh. Even if we did once know Christ in the flesh, that is not how we know him now. And for anyone who is in Christ, there is a new creation; the old creation has gone, and now the new one is here. It is all God's work. It was God who reconciled us to himself through Christ and gave us the work of handing on this reconciliation. In other words, God in Christ was reconciling the world to himself, not holding men's faults against them, and he has entrusted to us the news that they are reconciled. So we are ambassadors for Christ; it is as though God were appealing through us, and the appeal that we make in Christ's name is: be reconciled to God. For our sake God made the sinless one into sin, so that in him we might become the goodness of God.
>
> As his fellow workers, we beg you once again not to neglect the grace of God that you have received. For he says: 'At the favourable time, I have listened to you; on the day of salvation I came to your help.' Well, now is the favourable time; this is the day of salvation. (2 Cor. 5:16–6:2)

Baptism, then, brought with it a new way of life and a new community. It was a challenge to whoever professed their faith in Jesus as the Christ. Baptism in water helped people to feel cleansed of the past and renewed by the Spirit of the risen Christ.

There appears to be a refreshing simplicity about the early practice concerning baptism as outlined above. Inevitably, subsequent developments included more elaborate rituals and ceremonies.

REFLECTION

- Recent statistics have revealed some interesting trends concerning baptism and religious practice. What do you think of these statistics and how useful are they? How much attention should be paid to them?
- Baptismal practice in the early church seemed to place great emphasis on a change in life-style. Do you see this reflected in baptismal practice today? How important do you think it is?
- What are your own experiences and memories of baptismal celebrations you may have taken part in, attended, or heard about? What different expectations did people have?

The start of the catechumenate

As it grew the Christian Church became a victim of persecution and hostility. Over time, a simple profession of faith in Jesus Christ no longer sufficed for those wishing to join a Christian community that was now keen to test the seriousness of those who were interested. First of all, people had to find a sponsor from the community who would present them for baptism after a period of preparation which lasted two or three years. In that time, the sponsor would be able to ascertain whether the candidate was determined enough to change their way of life – hence, this formation was more ethical than doctrinal. Indeed, some people, such as prostitutes, gladiators, and soldiers, were requested to find a new profession before being presented for baptism. The sponsor also had to make sure, as far as possible, that there was little chance of apostasy (a Christian's public denial of Christ) from a candidate. The role of the sponsor became one of guaranteeing the reliability of a candidate and acting as a witness to their life-style. The third century document, *The Apostolic Tradition of Hippolytus*, talks of a three-year period of preparation, adding 'if a man be earnest and persevere well in the matter, let him be received, because it is not the time that is judged but the conduct'.

This lengthy period of preparation became known as the *catechumenate*, and those wishing to join the Christian community were known as *catechumens*. The term comes from the Greek for 'instruction'. In the time of the apostles we have seen that baptism occurred immediately after conversion, after the profession of faith in Jesus Christ. By the third century, baptism had become an annual celebration, usually linked to Easter (thus strengthening the theological link with the idea of death and resurrection to new life through the sacrament).

Preparation intensified as the annual celebration of baptism approached. Some weeks before baptism, the candidates were presented to the bishop or his representative by their sponsors, who testified to their worthiness for baptism. The bishop accepted them in the name of the Lord, and for the first time they began their doctrinal preparation. This took the form of instruction on Scripture and the creed. Every Sunday the candidates were also exorcised of the evil spirits of their past. In the week leading up to their Easter baptism, candidates received instruction on a daily basis. They were taught the Lord's Prayer and had to memorise the Apostles' Creed.

For the final two days before Easter, the candidates fasted from food. Then on the Vigil of Easter day, they gathered with the community to listen to the Word of God (similar to present Easter Vigils, with the Paschal Candle lit from the fire, and the Old Testament readings describing God's salvation for his people). At dawn, the candidates gathered at the baptismal pool. They recited the creed and the Lord's Prayer, renounced the devil, and were anointed with pre-baptismal oil, a sign of strength. The water was blessed by the bishop and the candidates went down naked into the pool or cistern. Three steps led to the bottom of the pool, and the candidates stood there in the water. 'Do you believe in God, the Father Almighty, the Creator of heaven and earth?', the bishop asked. 'I do believe,' was the reply, and the candidate was immersed in the water. 'Do you believe in Jesus Christ, his Son, our Lord, who was brought into the world to suffer for it?'; 'I do believe', the candidate replied before the second immersion. 'Do you believe in the Holy Spirit, the Holy Church, the resurrection of the body and life everlasting?'; 'I do believe' was followed by the third and final immersion.[3] The candidate then climbed out of the water, was anointed in the name of Christ, and presented with a white garment, which the newly-baptised would keep for a week. The bishop laid his hands on the candidates, praying that they might be filled with the Holy Spirit, and all the community continued with the celebration of the Eucharist, at which the newly-baptised participated for the first time.

At these celebrations the candidates received the sacraments of baptism, confirmation, and Eucharist. They became fully initiated members of the Christian community, and were surrounded by that community during the celebration. Throughout, there was emphasis on the break with the past and the beginning of new life. The sacrament of baptism filled the baptised with God's grace and the Holy Spirit, brought about the forgiveness of sins, and was not to be repeated. As Tertullian declared at the start of the third century:

> The body is washed so that the soul may be cleansed, the body is anointed so that the soul may be made holy, the body is marked with the sign of the cross so that the soul may be strengthened, the body receives the laying on of hands so that the soul may be enlightened by the Holy Spirit, the body is fed by the flesh and blood of Christ so that the soul may be nourished by God.[4]

In the year 313, the Emperor Constantine officially recognised the Christian religion. There was no longer any need to be secretive about Christian worship, or even being a Christian, and the number of baptisms increased. Christianity became the official religion of the Roman empire in 380, and Christians were favoured and protected by the Roman emperors. Therefore, it became almost fashionable to become a Christian, and some undoubtedly became Christians for motives that had little to do with faith.

As numbers in the Church grew, the bishops became more remote from their communities. Whereas before a bishop would be attached to his community in a town, the spread of Christianity into other areas meant that he lost touch with large numbers of people. It became the custom for the priest to baptise the candidates of his own community, and then wait for the bishop to visit for the laying on of hands, praying for the Holy Spirit to come down upon the candidates. (In 465, Faustus, Bishop of Riez, referred to this as 'confirmation'.)

Theological debate about the practices we have seen develop raised a number of questions and problems. Since penance for those who sinned after baptism was quite severe, and there was a belief that forgiveness could only be obtained once, it became common practice to delay baptism until near death. People chose to remain catechumens for as long as possible, and the number of death-bed conversions increased. If catechumens failed to be baptised before death, they still hoped for salvation because of their desire for baptism.

As regards children, a similar problem arose. If baptism was necessary for salvation, what was the fate of those children who died unbaptised, a distinct possibility given the high infant mortality rate? The solution for many parents was to baptise children as soon as possible after birth, rather than waiting for the annual baptismal celebration at Easter. Gradually, the practice of infant baptism as soon as possible after birth became accepted. The reason was provided by Cyprian of Carthage (d. 258), who said an infant needed forgiveness for the 'sin of Adam', washed away in baptism. His idea was based largely on a passage from St Paul's letter to the Romans (cf. 5:12–21), where it states: 'As by one man's disobedience many were made sinners, so by one man's obedience many will be made righteous' (5:19).

St Augustine provided a more detailed explanation of this nearly 150 years later, stating that from the moment of conception we have the sin of Adam on our soul. He provided us with the concept of *original sin*, describing it as a spiritual deformity present in the soul from birth. We are reshaped through the baptismal seal of Christ: 'Why would it be necessary to form the little child in a figure of Christ's death through baptism if he were not already poisoned by the serpent's bite?'[5] Original sin was transmitted through the father, who passed on something of his body and soul to his child, who thus inherited not just a father's physical characteristics but also his sinful nature. Augustine went further, and declared that infants who died without baptism would be damned, although their punishment would be mild (since they had not actually committed any sins). Eventually, in the Middle Ages a popular tradition arose whereby infants who died without baptism went to *limbo* – a state of natural happiness, but not heaven. The Catholic Church has never taught this as part of its doctrine.*

By the end of the fifth century, infant baptism had become the norm, and it was not necessarily reserved for the Easter Vigil. This meant, of course, that the catechumenate, that period of moral preparation, disappeared, as did the doctrinal preparation that immediately preceded the Easter baptismal celebration. The need for faith in the one to be baptised was supplied by the sponsor, who spoke on the infant's behalf. The role of the sponsor thus underwent a change: rather than being a guarantor of the candidate's faith and way of life, the sponsor now became a guardian of the child's faith after baptism, responsible for the Christian upbringing of the child. The increase in infant baptism also brought about a very practical change: total immersion was no longer feasible and so pouring water over the child's head became the norm (although in the Eastern Churches total immersion remained), as the minister pronounced the words: 'I baptise you in the name of the Father, and of the Son, and of the Holy Spirit'.

* The *Catechism of the Catholic Church* states: 'As regards children who have died without Baptism, the Church can only entrust them to the mercy of God, as she does in her funeral rites for them. Indeed, the great mercy of God who desires that all men should be saved, and Jesus' tenderness towards children which caused him to say: "Let the children come to me, do not hinder them", allow us to hope that there is a way of salvation for children who have died without Baptism. All the more urgent is the Church's call not to prevent little children coming to Christ through the gift of holy Baptism,' n. 1261. There is a view that the notion of limbo arose simply out of confusion. The word means 'margin' or 'periphery', and the original answer concerning the fate of the unbaptised infant was to place the problem *in the margin*, because the answer was not known. By some mistake, *in the margin*, in limbo, became a technical term for a place for unbaptised children who had died.

REFLECTION

- The initial period of preparation in the catechumenate examined a candidate's ability to live a Christian life, with the need to change job if necessary. It was ethical/moral preparation rather than doctrinal. How important do you think this is? Should moral preparation precede or follow doctrinal instruction?
- The role of the sponsor or godparent has changed. How do you view that change? Have you ever acted as a sponsor or godparent? Why were you asked and what has it meant to you?
- Baptism gradually became associated with infants, probably arising out of a fear of unbaptised infants not going to heaven. Do you think this was a good motive for baptism and do you think this idea might persist today?
- The initial celebration of 'baptism' at the Easter Vigil was, as we have seen, the celebration of what are now three distinct sacraments: baptism, confirmation, and Eucharist (although in the Eastern Churches infants receive the three sacraments together). What do you think of this? Should the three sacraments be celebrated together, or is it better to separate them as they are now?

Further developments

From the sixth century, the baptism of infants was the norm. There was a shift, too, in the sacramental emphasis. Baptism was now seen as washing away original sin and promising eternal life; gone was any emphasis on the beginning of a new life. There was a complete separation of baptism and confirmation: the priest baptised in his local community, and that baptism was 'confirmed' by the bishop at his next visit, when he laid on hands and anointed those who had been baptised by the priest. This second anointing was reserved to the bishop, who thereby 'confirmed' earlier baptisms.

In many areas of Europe baptism still took place at Easter, and so 'confirmation' would take place some time afterwards.

But with infant mortality on the increase some bishops actually advised parents not to wait until Easter for baptism. Gradually, baptism soon after birth was positively encouraged until finally it became church law that infants should be baptised very soon after birth to save them from the trauma of dying still stained with original sin. A church document from 1442 actually sets a time limit:

> With regard to children, on account of the danger of death which can occur, since no other remedy can help them than the sacrament of baptism by which they are snatched away from the devil's dominion and made the adopted sons of God . . . [the Church] warns that holy baptism should not be delayed for forty or eighty days, or for some other length of time according to the custom observed by some; but it must be conferred as soon as can suitably be done, with the provision that, if the peril of death is imminent, the children be baptised at once without any delay, even, if no priest is available, by a layman or a woman . . .[6]

In terms of the ritual itself, this had now been completely separated from the Easter Vigil. Baptism became a private ceremony, with the parents and godparents in attendance, and a standard baptismal formula: 'I baptise you, in the name of the Father, and of the Son, and of the Holy Spirit', accompanied by a triple pouring of water on the infant's head. In many respects, the elaborate initiation ritual celebrated in the early Christian communities had been stripped bare, to a simple, private celebration of one sacrament alone, baptism.

In their love of order, scholastic theologians of the twelfth and thirteenth century tried to define the 'matter' (the materials and gestures of the rite) and 'form' (the significance) of baptism. Hugh of St Victor (d. 1142) defined baptism as 'water made holy by the word of God for washing away sins'.[7] For Thomas Aquinas, the 'matter' of the sacrament was the water, while the 'form' was expressed in the Trinitarian formula, 'I baptise you in the name of the Father, and of the Son, and of the Holy Spirit'. The sacrament set the baptised on the Christian path. For Aquinas, the sacrament had two effects: in the soul of the baptised the rite produced a sacramental reality, the seal or image of Christ (the sacramental character), and baptism enabled the human spirit to rise above its natural abilities to be more Christ-like, to show the virtues of faith, hope, and love. For Aquinas, the secondary effect of baptism was the exercise of these virtues. This made baptism very much a two-way process: God conferred these virtues, but people needed to co-operate in using them to resist temptation, to try to lead a good life. Salvation, then, was a matter in which the baptised needed to co-operate with God. And the start of that process of co-operation was baptism.

As scholastic theologians continued to debate matters such as the role of faith, grace, and the sacramental character, for many ordinary people the baptism of infants became almost a magical ritual. Something happened to the soul of the baptised infant, and the effect was purely spiritual. The social consequences were that it made the baptised a member of a faith community.

The debate continued in the time of the Reformation, with Martin Luther in particular focusing on the role of faith and grace. He believed that sacraments were signs of God's grace, but they did not have any effect until that grace was consciously accepted in faith. In these terms, faith was not a question of doctrinal assent but a relationship based on love of God. Baptism of infants was acceptable, for, as Luther stated, 'my faith does not constitute baptism but receives it'.[8] The Anabaptists adopted a fundamental biblical position, arguing that the New Testament only spoke of adult baptism which required a profession of faith, and therefore infant baptism was meaningless. As regards forgiveness of sin, Luther argued that baptism brought God's forgiveness, even though the baptised might continue to sin.

The Catholic Church's response to what were seen as Protestant heresies came once again at the Council of Trent in the middle of the sixteenth century. No doctrinal statement on baptism was issued, but the heretical positions of Luther, Calvin and other reformers were condemned.

4. If anyone says that baptism, even that given by heretics in the name of the Father and of the Son and of the Holy Spirit, with the intention of doing what the Church does, is not true baptism, *anathema sit*.
5. If anyone says that baptism is optional, that is, not necessary for salvation, *anathema sit*.
6. If anyone says that one baptised cannot lose grace, even if he wishes to, no matter how much he sins, unless he is unwilling to believe, *anathema sit*.
7. If anyone says that those baptised are by the fact of their baptism obliged merely to faith alone, but not to the observance of the whole law of Christ, *anathema sit*.
13. If anyone says that because little children do not have actual faith, they are not to be numbered among the faithful after receiving baptism, and that, for this reason, they are to be re-baptised when they have reached the age of discretion; or that it is better to omit their baptism rather than to baptise them solely in the faith of the Church while they do not believe by an act of their own, *anathema sit*.[9]

Although the Council of Trent set out in strong language the Catholic Church's belief and practice concerning baptism, nevertheless the sacrament remained for most people a magic ritual. It had reached the stage where it made little practical difference to people's lives.

'Baptism of desire'

One of the more important ideas developed by scholastic theologians was that of 'baptism of desire'. Thomas Aquinas had said that prior to the coming of Christ it was sufficient to believe in God in order to receive the effects of baptism. Some theologians said this in itself was an implicit faith in the Christ who was to come. Thomas modified this popular view and added that with the coming of Christ an explicit profession of faith was required in order to receive the effects of baptism.

As the Americas and the Far East were discovered, the question of salvation for the whole of humanity became more urgent among theologians. What about those in these 'new worlds' who had not heard the message of Christ? It was held that faith in God was an implicit acknowledgement of Jesus, and therefore counted as 'baptism of desire'. This idea emphasised the notion that Christ was the unique mediator of salvation and that his grace could touch the heart of everyone with an invitation calling for a response. It was an acknowledgement that God was working for the salvation of all both within the Church and also outside it. 'Baptism of desire' may not welcome people into a specific community, but it does reflect the idea that all holiness and goodness is rooted in God.

In this century, the idea 'baptism of desire' is used in reference to people who, through no fault of their own, have not heard of the saving message of Christ, and yet lead good lives. Surely, it is argued, such people would not be punished by God. The fact that they had not heard the Gospel message is the 'fault' of the Church (if fault is the right term to use in such a context), because the Church has not managed to bring the Gospel to them. At the Second Vatican Council, 'baptism of desire' referred to those people who, 'through no fault of their own, do not know the Gospel of Christ or his Church, but who nevertheless seek God with a sincere heart, and, moved by grace, try in their actions to do his will as they know it through the dictates of their conscience – these too may attain eternal salvation'.[10] The step taken by the bishops at the Council cannot be underestimated here: the notion being expressed is that baptism is necessary for joining the Church, but not necessary for salvation.

Baptism today

As was noted in the introductory chapter on sacramental theology, the Second Vatican Council was not a surprise event sprung upon the Catholic Church without a moment's notice. It was, rather, part of a process, a process that included increased biblical and historical scholarship. This had an important effect on how the sacrament of baptism was viewed.

There was a return to St Paul's image of dying and rising with Christ through baptism:

> Thus by Baptism men and women are implanted in the paschal mystery of Christ; they die with him, are buried with him, and rise with him. They receive the spirit of adoption as sons and daughters 'in which we cry, Abba, Father' (Rom. 8:15) and thus become true adorers such as the Father seeks.[11]

> By his power he [Christ] is present in the sacraments so that when anybody baptises it is really Christ himself who baptises.[12]

> In this body [the Church] the life of Christ is communicated to those who believe and who, through the sacraments, are united in a hidden and real way to Christ in his passion and glorification. Through Baptism we are formed in the likeness of Christ: 'For in one Spirit we were all baptised into one body' (1 Cor. 12:13). In this sacred rite our union with Christ's death and resurrection is symbolised and effected: 'For we were buried with him by Baptism into death'; and if 'we have been united with him in the likeness of his death, we shall be so in the likeness of his resurrection also' (Rom. 6:4–5).[13]

In ecumenical terms, the Council declared:

> By the sacrament of Baptism, whenever it is properly conferred in the way the Lord determined and received with the proper dispositions of soul, people become truly incorporated into the crucified and glorified Christ . . . Baptism . . . establishes a sacramental bond of unity among all who through it are reborn.[14]

> . . . one cannot charge with the sin of the separation those who at present are born into these [separated] communities and in them are brought up in the faith of Christ, and the Catholic Church accepts them with respect and affection as brothers and sisters. For those who believe in Christ

and have been properly baptised are put in some, though imperfect, communion with the Catholic Church.[15]*

The bishops called for a revision of baptismal rites, and in 1969 the revised *Rite of Baptism for Children* was published. The emphasis has now gone back to being welcomed into a Christian community and living a new life of faith. The Introduction states that the 'people of God, that is the Church, made present by the local community, has an important part to play in the baptism of both children and adults'.[16] The Rite itself begins with the minister signing the cross on the forehead of the child to be baptised, saying: '*N.*, the Christian community welcomes you with great joy. In its name I claim you for Christ our Saviour by the sign of his cross. I now trace the cross on your forehead and invite your parents and godparents to do the same.' The community's involvement can be seen today in the many baptisms that take place during a Sunday Mass, in the presence of the Christian community. The role of parents and godparents has also received extra emphasis, with the first question in the Rite being: 'You have asked to have your child baptised. In doing so you are accepting the responsibility of training him (her) in the practice of the faith. It will be your duty to bring him (her) up to keep God's commandments as Christ taught us, by loving God and our neighbour. Do you clearly understand what you are undertaking?' In practical terms this often results in baptism preparation courses, where parents and godparents may be asked to attend a number of meetings prior to baptism. This is a massive shift from the almost magical view of baptism common in earlier centuries, where baptism was seen as an automatic step in the life of a child.†

The entire vision of initiation in the Catholic Church today was given fresh impetus in 1972 with the publication of the

* In 1971 the Catholic Bishops of England and Wales issued a statement accepting 'in principle the Baptism of non-Catholic Churches whose baptismal rite is recognised as valid . . . [that is] Baptism administered with the application of water in the name of the Father and of the Son and of the Holy Spirit'.

† In 1980, a Vatican *Instruction on Infant Baptism* went further and suggested that if parents could give no assurances that a child would be brought up as a Catholic, then 'it will be prudent to delay baptism'.

Rite of Christian Initiation of Adults (R.C.I.A.). In many respects this was a return to the early Church model of initiation, a process whereby adults would enter into the Christian community. The process is divided into stages, with each stage marked by a special rite: Stage of Inquiry (pre-catechumenate, ending with the Rite of Entry), the Catechumenate (a formation period of indeterminate length, ending with the Rite of Election on the first Sunday of Lent), a Period of Purification and Enlightenment (concluding with reception into the Church at the Easter Vigil), and the Period of Mystagogia (a time for learning more about the faith embraced and entering further into the life of the community). The R.C.I.A. may take many years, and an inquirer is, of course, free to decide whether or not to continue along this path of Christian initiation. Without entering into all the details of the R.C.I.A., what this process does reveal is that the Catholic Church views initiation as not simply doctrinal instruction, but a process of conversion which has spiritual, theological and moral effects.

Conclusion

Baptism preparation courses, R.C.I.A. as the norm for Christian initiation – these point to a major shift in the understanding of baptism today. It is not a magical ritual which has an invisible effect on the one who is baptised, child or adult. It is not simply a social convention, or a performance to be gone through in order to guarantee a school place.

In the eyes of the Church, baptism is the start of a new way of life. Sometimes, an adult will come to that view after years of prayer and reflection; sometimes parents will declare, on behalf of a child, that they hope to be 'the best of teachers' in this way of life. Yes, baptism does wash away original sin, but that is only the start. Baptism is a challenge. The baptised will be formed by, and will help to form the community into which they are welcomed – and so each one of us must surely have a role to play in every baptism in our community.

REFLECTION

- Infant baptism eventually became a private celebration. Why do you think this was so? What were the benefits and disadvantages?
- 'Outside the Church there is no salvation' – what image of God do you think this offers? 'Baptism of desire' – what image of God does this suggest? If we accept 'baptism of desire' is there any need to be baptised? Is it better to be an 'anonymous Christian'?
- Many parishes now insist that parents and godparents attend a 'Baptism Preparation Course'. Is this right? The parents may then be told that the baptism will take place during Sunday Mass. Wouldn't it be better in the afternoon when a crying baby will disturb fewer people?
- Is the Church right to encourage delaying baptism?
- What were the good and not so good aspects of any baptisms (adult or infant) that you may have attended or heard about recently?
- How does the Church encourage a sense of 'belonging to a Christian community' today? Do you feel welcome? Is there anything else the Church could do to improve that sense of 'belonging'?
- If baptism is a challenge to us all, how do we respond?

Baptism is God's most beautiful and magnificent gift . . .
We call it gift, grace, anointing, enlightenment
garment of immortality, bath of rebirth, seal
and most precious gift.
It is called gift
because it is conferred
on those who bring nothing of their own;
grace *since it is given even to the guilty;*
Baptism *because sin is buried in the water;*
anointing *for it is priestly and royal*
as those who are anointed;
enlightenment *because it radiates light;*

clothing *since it veils our shame;*
bath *because it washes;*
and seal *as it is our guard and the sign of God's Lordship.*

(St Gregory of Nazianzus)[17]

4 *Confirmation*

A recently published preparation programme for the sacrament of confirmation bears the interesting title *Survival Guide to Confirmation.*[1] The front cover shows a priest dragging two youngsters by the scruff of the neck. Their destination: Confirmation Class! The introduction states:

> At this stage it is worth noting that the programme makes two major assumptions: 1. That the candidate is not interested in religion, does not want to attend Confirmation classes and is personally not bothered about receiving the Sacrament. 2. That the catechist is relatively inexperienced at running Confirmation classes.[2]

This may seem a negative picture to paint, but sadly it is all too real. For many, confirmation can be a sacrament marking the end of both formal religious education and any real involvement with the Church – a sacrament of 'exit' rather than a confirmation of earlier promises. Of course, this is not the only picture. There are many people for whom the sacrament is *really* a confirmation of their faith, and there are many catechists who devote much time and energy to handing on that faith.

There are many questions raised by the sacrament of confirmation and in particular its relation to baptism. The sacrament of baptism is not just about forgiveness of sins and being welcomed into the Christian community, it is a sacrament of rebirth, of being filled with the Spirit. But confirmation also hands on the Spirit: 'Send your Holy Spirit [on these candidates] to be their Helper and Guide.'[3] Who is the sacrament for: adults, adolescents, infants? Should it take place at the very start of someone's life in the Christian community or some years later? And in being confirmed what is the Christian becoming, what stage of faith do they pass through? Such questions arising from centuries of varied practices have prompted many scholars to refer to confirmation as a 'sacrament in search of a theology'. What do we *really* understand by confirmation?

Christian initiation

In the early Church someone professed their acceptance of Christ and openness to the Spirit through baptism. They were welcomed into the Christian community and received the spirit of Christ: '. . . You have been washed clean, and sanctified, and justified through the name of the Lord Jesus Christ and through the Spirit of our God. . . . Your body, you know, is the temple of the Holy Spirit, who is in you since you received him from God' (1 Cor. 6:11, 19); 'I tell you most solemnly, unless a man is born through water and the Spirit, he cannot enter the kingdom of God' (John 3:5).

Jesus himself had spoken of the Spirit, the helper whom he would send:

> If you love me you will keep my commandments. I shall ask the Father and he will give you another Advocate to be with you for ever, that Spirit of truth whom the world can never receive since it neither sees nor knows him; but you know him, because he is with you, he is in you . . . the Advocate, the Holy Spirit, whom the Father will send in my name, will teach you everything and remind you of all I have said to you. (John 14:15–17, 26)

The Acts of the Apostles provides the well-known account of the 'on-rushing' of the Spirit on the day traditionally called the 'birthday of the Church':

> When Pentecost day came round, they had all met in one room, when suddenly they heard what sounded like a powerful wind from heaven, the noise of which filled the entire house in which they were sitting; and something appeared to them that seemed like tongues of fire; these separated and came to rest on the head of each of them. They were all filled with the Holy Spirit, and began to

> speak foreign languages as the Spirit gave them the gift of speech. (Acts 2:1–4)

This event changed those who received the Spirit: they formed a close-knit community, they witnessed to their faith, and many of those they met asked to be baptised.

Although it is difficult to identify precise practices in the early Church, there is evidence suggesting that at baptism a person was washed clean of sin, received the Holy Spirit, and was welcomed into the Christian community. The Pentecost story mentioned above continues with Peter's message to the crowds: 'You must repent and every one of you must be baptised in the name of Jesus Christ for the forgiveness of your sins, and you will receive the gift of the Holy Spirit' (Acts 2:38).

Other texts suggest that the practice of 'laying on of hands' was significant:

> When the apostles in Jerusalem heard that Samaria had accepted the word of God, they sent Peter and John to them, and they went down there, and prayed for the Samaritans to receive the Holy Spirit, for as yet he had not come down on any of them: they had only been baptised in the name of the Lord Jesus. Then they laid hands on them and they received the Holy Spirit. (Acts 8:14–17)

In Ephesus, Paul finds a group of people who 'were never even told there was such a thing as a Holy Spirit'. They had only received John's baptism, and so they 'were baptised in the name of the Lord Jesus, and the moment Paul had laid hands on them the Holy Spirit came down on them, and they began to speak with tongues and to prophesy' (Acts 19:1–7).

The evidence of the New Testament and early Church experience suggests that baptism was one process of initiation which included receiving the Holy Spirit. Adults were welcomed into the Christian community at the Easter Vigil. After immersion in the pool at this ceremony, the candidate was anointed in the name of Christ. The bishop would lay his hands on the candidate, praying that he/she might be filled with the Holy Spirit. The whole community then continued with the celebration of the Eucharist, at which the newly-baptised participated for the first time. Initiation had developed from a simple ritual with water to a complex ritual which was the culmination of a lengthy period of preparation. That ritual included a number of different aspects, with prayers, washings, and anointings: 'Then having come up from the font we are thoroughly anointed with a blessed unction . . . In the next place the hand is laid on in blessing, invoking and inviting the Holy Spirit' writes Tertullian in about the year 200.[4]

It would seem that by about this time there was one ritual of initiation with two elements: a cleansing with water and a rite for receiving the Holy Spirit. The key figure in further development was to become the local bishop.

<u>*REFLECTION*</u>

- Confirmation has been called a 'sacrament of exit'. What are your memories of confirmation – for yourself, family, friends, or any confirmations you have heard about? What is your initial reaction to the sacrament of confirmation?
- How aware are you of preparation for confirmation? What do you think it is trying to do? What guidelines for the sacrament are you aware of (e.g. age, who can be confirmed, who can confirm, when is the celebration to take place)?
- Looking at the evidence of the New Testament and the early Church, can you see how the separate rites of initiation developed? What do you think are the advantages and disadvantages?

The bishop

At the Easter Vigil, the local bishop laid hands on or extended his hands over newly-baptised members of the community, invoking upon them the gift of the Holy Spirit. Then he anointed them with consecrated oil, made the sign of the cross on their forehead, and gave them the kiss of peace. The bishop's action was seen as a sign of the candidates' acceptance into the Christian community. He represented not only that local community but also the wider Church, and so his presence was essential.

Among scholars, there was debate about precisely when people received the Holy Spirit. Tertullian believed it was at the laying on of hands, while Ambrose (*c.* 339–97), Bishop of Milan, stated that at baptism Christians received the gift of new life and forgiveness through water and the Spirit, and at the imposition of hands they received the gifts of the Holy Spirit mentioned in the prophet Isaiah: 'A shoot springs from the stock of Jesse, a scion thrusts from his roots: on him the spirit of Yahweh rests, a spirit of wisdom and insight, a spirit of counsel and power, a spirit of knowledge and of the fear of Yahweh' (Isaiah 11:1–2).

Irrespective of the precise moment when the Spirit was conferred upon a candidate, be it at baptism or later, it was clear that at the end of the initiation ritual the Spirit had been conferred. But as the number of baptisms grew and the communities increased, it became more difficult for the bishop to be present at every celebration. Numbers rose dramatically after Theodosius made Christianity the official religion of the Roman Empire in 380, and so increasingly bishops could not initiate all members into their local Christian community.

The response to this varied. In many Eastern Churches priests were given authority to act in the bishop's name and carry out the complete rite of initiation. For the anointing they used oil that had been consecrated by the bishop and so symbolised his presence. Western Churches, however, continued to insist on the need for the bishop to complete the initiation of Christians in person. The Council of Elvira, in Spain, declared at the start of the fourth century that a catechumen baptised by one of the faithful in case of sickness must be brought 'to the bishop that he may be perfected by the imposition of hand'.[5] In 416 Pope Innocent I distinguished clearly between baptism, which included an anointing with chrism and was performed by a priest, and what he termed the 'signing' (*consignatio*) with chrism reserved for the bishop. Writing to the Bishop of Gubbio in Italy he referred to the passage we have already seen in the Acts of the Apostles where Peter and John were directed to confer the Holy Spirit on the people of Samaria (Acts 8:14–17):

> For it is allowed to presbyters when they baptise either in the absence of the bishop or in his presence to anoint with chrism those who are being baptised, though only with chrism consecrated by the bishop; but not to sign their forehead with the same oil, which is reserved to the bishops when they confer the Spirit the Paraclete.[6]

Slowly, what was to become known as confirmation was reserved to the bishop alone. The rite was really one of 'consignation', as the signing of the candidate's forehead with the sign of the cross replaced the laying on of hands. This anointing was seen as completing baptism, and is still in force in Orthodox baptisms. Here the infant is 'chrismated' after baptism, and before being given communion. It is an anointing with the sign of the cross on the child's forehead, eyes, nostrils, lips, ears, breast, hands, and feet, saying each time: 'The seal of the gift of the Holy Spirit.' The term 'confirmation' was first used at the French Councils of Riez and Orange in 439 and 441. Priests were given permission to anoint the children they baptised with consecrated chrism, and bishops were later to confirm these baptisms by the imposition of hands.

Many people, however, saw little point in making an extra journey to have their child confirmed. In practice, there was a general belief that confirmation made little difference, and so many children were not confirmed. To counteract this trend, one French bishop spoke of the need for confirmation to make people more fully Christians. In confirmation, the Holy Spirit gave strength for the battle against sin.

Sacramental practice still varied throughout Europe. In the presence of a bishop, Christian initiation, involving baptism, confirmation, and Eucharist, was still given to adults and children. Or where fear of dying without baptism was strong, infants were baptised by their local priest without confirmation by the bishop in later years. Many people still needed to be convinced of the necessity of confirmation. It was argued that baptism was necessary for salvation, so what could confirmation by a bishop add?

The situation was to undergo another change thanks to a collection of genuine and forged documents made in France and today known as the *False Decretals*. The documents were attributed to Isidore of Seville (d. 636), and contained forged letters from Pope Urban I (pope from 222–30) and Pope Melchiades (a non-existent pope), a group of genuine and forged letters from the popes of the fourth to the eighth century, and a collection of canons from some Church Councils, mostly genuine. The purpose of the *False Decretals* was to defend the rights of diocesan bishops, and in terms of confirmation it was made clear people should receive the sacrament through the bishop's imposition of hands in order to make them fully Christians. Another forged letter in the collection spoke of the Holy Spirit given at confirmation for combat against evil. Surprisingly enough, the *False Decretals* were accepted as genuine throughout Europe and were seen as authoritative practice.

From the ninth century onwards, therefore, the custom of the bishop's confirmation was adopted throughout Europe. On his visitation to a parish, the bishop confirmed those who had been baptised, although by now it was not just the baptisms of the previous Easter, but the baptisms of a number of years, since baptism was no longer limited to just Easter and the bishop did not manage to visit the growing numbers of parishes each year. Parts of today's rite of confirmation can be traced to this period. William Durandus, who became Bishop of Mende in France in 1285, was one of the most important liturgists of his time, and in confirmation he changed the imposition of hands on each candidate to an extension of the hand over all the candidates. Bishop Durandus also introduced one of the most memorable aspects of confirmation – the slap on the cheek, a sign that in this sacrament the candidate received strength to fight temptation.

For scholastic theologians of the thirteenth century confirmation was necessary because Christians were obliged to defend themselves against temptation. Thomas Aquinas saw confirmation as necessary for achieving spiritual perfection with the aid of the Holy Spirit. The scholastic debate on 'matter' and 'form' (the concrete elements of a ritual and the meaning attached to it) was resolved in terms of confirmation with the 'matter' being the anointing with chrism, and the 'form' the formula pronounced by the bishop as he anointed. The standard formula in the thirteenth century was: 'I sign you with the sign of the cross, and I confirm you with the chrism of salvation, in the name of the Father and of the Son and of the Holy Spirit.'

Also up for debate by scholastic theologians was the institution of the sacrament. Some said confirmation was instituted by the apostles, while others pointed to various parts of the New Testament where Christ may have instituted the sacrament (e.g. 'After saying this he breathed on them and said: "Receive the Holy Spirit." ' John 20:22). Thomas Aquinas said that Christ instituted the sacrament of confirmation by promising it: 'I shall ask the Father, and he will give you another Advocate to be with you for ever, that Spirit of truth whom the world can never receive since it neither sees nor knows him; but you know him, because he is with you, he is in you' (John 14:17).

As a sacrament confirmation was given only once, and so like baptism it bestowed a sacramental character. This character had to be different from the one given in baptism. Aquinas stated that the character of baptism enabled Christians to achieve salvation; in the character of confirmation they received the power to attain spiritual perfection and to fight temptation. In a sense, one sacrament was about spiritual birth, the other about spiritual growth. Debate also focused on the gifts of the Holy Spirit as another way of distinguishing baptism and confirmation. It was argued that at baptism one received the Holy Spirit and in confirmation one received the seven gifts of that Spirit: wisdom, understanding, counsel, fortitude, knowledge, piety, and the fear of the Lord.

As regards the age of confirmation, we have seen that by now baptism was completely separated from confirmation. Since the emphasis in confirmation was on strength in the fight against temptation and public witness of the faith, confirmation of infants was becoming questionable. The traditional practice was confirmation as soon as possible after baptism, usually by the age of one or two (and in some cases parents who neglected to have their children confirmed by this age were fined). Gradually, the age for confirmation went up. The 'age of discretion' became the acceptable age for the sacrament, on the grounds that the graces of confirmation were not needed until a child could distinguish between right and wrong – again the sacramental emphasis would seem to be the fight against temptation. Of course, the next problem was when did somebody reach the 'age of discretion'? Official statements on this are rare, although one Church Council in 1280 said that children under seven should not be confirmed and other local decrees put the age for confirmation at 12 or 14.

But in 1439 the practice and theology of confirmation was clearly stated at the Council of Florence. This Council declared that the ordinary minister of the sacrament was the bishop:

> For we read that only the apostles, whose place the bishops hold, imparted the Holy Spirit by the laying on of hand [see Acts 8:14–17] . . . Confirmation given by the Church takes the place of that imposition of hand . . . The effect of this sacrament is that in it the Holy Spirit is given for strength, as He was given to the apostles on the day of Pentecost, in order that the Christian may courageously confess the name of Christ. And, therefore, the one to be confirmed is anointed on the forehead which is the seat of shame, so that he may not be ashamed to confess the name of Christ, and chiefly His cross, which, according to the apostle, is a stumbling block for the Jews and foolishness for the gentiles. This is why he is signed with the sign of the cross.[7]

It was also acknowledged that priests might be delegated to perform confirmation provided they used the chrism blessed by the bishop.

REFLECTION

- Confirmation was encouraged because it was said to make people more fully Christians. Do you think this is still true today? In what way might it be true?
- The 'age of discretion' was seen as the right moment for confirmation. How would you define the 'age of discretion' and how would you apply it to confirmation?
- The role of the bishop is central to confirmation. What do

you think is the importance of his role in the celebration of the sacrament?

- In *Doors to the Sacred* Joseph Martos sums up confirmation in the Middle Ages in this way: 'Legally Catholics were obliged to be confirmed, although few could specify exactly why. Theologically it did not seem to make any difference in a person's ability to get to heaven, and morally it did not seem to make any difference in a person's life. Moreover, bishops sometimes used confirmation in the various parishes around their diocese as an opportunity to put on a show of episcopal dignity, and to take up a collection.' Any comments?

Confirmation and the reformers

The Protestant reformers' response to what they saw happening in confirmation was blunt. It was held to have no basis in Scripture, was not instituted by Christ, and was a denial of the fact that the Holy Spirit was received at baptism.

Martin Luther stated that confirmation was in fact a simple church ceremony similar to the blessing of water. He accepted that such a ritual could be retained only if its purpose was pastoral: 'I can see nothing wrong', he said in 1533, 'if every pastor would examine the faith of the children to see whether it is good and sincere, lay hands on them and confirm them.'

Although a number of Protestant churches abolished confirmation it was retained by the Church of England. In 1549 it stopped confirming infants, but said that children should be confirmed prior to their first communion. In preparation for confirmation children were to be instructed and examined in the catechism. The second edition of the *Book of Common Prayer* (1552) prescribed the rite of confirmation as the imposition of hands by the bishop (rather than the signing on the forehead), who prayed that the candidates would be courageous in professing their faith in Christ and continue to be Christ's faithful soldiers.

The Catholic Church's response to these Protestant ideas was equally blunt. The Council of Trent (1547) declared: 'If anyone says that the confirmation of those baptised is a useless ceremony and not a true and proper sacrament; or that of old it was nothing more than a sort of catechesis in which those nearing adolescence gave an account of their faith before the Church, *anathema sit.*' The *Catechism* of the Council of Trent, published in 1556, was more expansive on the sacrament of confirmation. It stated that the sacrament could be given to any baptised Catholic, that it was unnecessary to be confirmed before the age of seven, but confirmation should not be postponed beyond the age of 12. In practice, the sacrament continued to be given before First Communion (partly due to the fact that the age for receiving First Communion had been put back).

The theology and practice of confirmation remained unaltered thereafter for some time. Now and again there were minor alterations in the rite of confirmation. Nearly three hundred years after the Council of Trent some Catholic churches began to give communion before confirmation, especially in France. This was more due to a developing understanding of communion than any theological development of confirmation. This practice was approved in 1910 by Pope Pius X, who encouraged children to receive communion from the age of seven. Communion before confirmation became the norm, and thus confirmation was completely separated from baptism and Eucharist as a sacrament of initiation. The unique process of initiation that we saw at the time of the early Church had been completely broken up. This development raised the inevitable, and perhaps still unanswered question: if participation at the Eucharist is the sign of full reception into the Church, where does that leave confirmation?

Confirmation today

The notion that confirmation is 'a sacrament in search of a theology' is now truer than ever before. In this century emphases have shifted: from confirmation as conferring the seven gifts of the Holy Spirit to confirmation as the sacrament which makes young people suddenly become active soldiers for Christ, ready to bring his message to the disbelieving world; or it has been seen as the sacrament which completes baptism (thereby affirming the Eastern Orthodox Church's practice of confirmation immediately after baptism); or as the sacrament whereby the candidate is accepted not just into the Christian community of his/her parish, but the wider community of the diocese and universal Church, represented by the bishop.

The connection between confirmation and the Holy Spirit is obvious. The bishop prays

> that [our Father] will pour out the Holy Spirit to strengthen his sons and daughters with his gifts and anoint them to be more like Christ the Son of God . . . Send your Holy Spirit upon them to be their Helper and Guide. Give them the spirit of wisdom and understanding, the spirit of right judgement and courage, the spirit of knowledge and reverence. Fill them with the spirit of wonder and awe in your presence.[8]

It seems that confirmation is a call to live by God's Spirit.

Where confirmation is conferred at a later age, the sacrament has clear connotations of Christian maturity. The candidates are acknowledging their adult commitment to faith, literally 'confirming' the promises made on their behalf at baptism. There is also an acknowledgement on the part of the Christian community that a mature commitment has been made in response to the call to become adult disciples in the world. With this in mind confirmation is also to be seen as a sacrament which strengthens, enabling those confirmed to undertake the responsibilities of discipleship today.

At the Second Vatican Council, the world's Catholic bishops called for a revision of confirmation, 'so that the intimate connection of this sacrament with the whole of Christian initiation may be shown more clearly'.[9] However, other Council texts referring to confirmation talk about strengthening by the Holy Spirit: 'By the sacrament of confirmation [the faithful] are more perfectly bound to the Church and are endowed with the special strength of the Holy Spirit. Hence, as true witnesses of Christ, they are more strictly obliged both to spread and to defend the faith by word and deed.'[10] 'Lay people's right and duty to be apostles derives from their union with Christ their head. Inserted as they are in the mystical body of Christ by baptism and strengthened by the power of the Holy Spirit in confirmation, it is by the Lord himself that they are assigned to the apostolate.'[11] Clearly there are two aspects to confirmation: the completion of Christian initiation and the strengthening through the Holy Spirit.

The theology of confirmation received another expression in the preface to the revised rite of the sacrament published under Pope Paul VI in 1971:

> Through the sacrament of confirmation, those who have been born anew in baptism receive the inexpressible Gift, the Holy Spirit himself, by which 'they are endowed . . . with special strength'. Moreover, having been signed with the character of this sacrament, they are 'more closely bound to the Church' and 'they are more strictly obliged to spread and defend the faith, both by word and deed, as true witnesses of Christ'. Finally, confirmation is so closely linked with the holy Eucharist that the faithful, after being signed by baptism and confirmation, are incorporated fully into the Body of Christ by participation in the Eucharist.[12]

Pope Paul VI decreed that the sacrament was to be conferred 'through the anointing with chrism on the forehead, which is done by the laying on of the hand, and through the words: "Be sealed with the Gift of the Holy Spirit." ' Significantly, bishops were also encouraged to allow priests in mission lands and priests who receive adults into the Church to administer the sacrament of confirmation.[13]

The *Catechism of the Catholic Church* refers to the effect of confirmation as the 'full outpouring of the Holy Spirit as once granted to the apostles on the day of Pentecost.'[14] It goes on to talk of an increase and deepening of baptismal grace:

> It roots us more deeply in the divine filiation which makes us cry *'Abba!* Father!'; it unites us more firmly to Christ; it increases the gifts of the Holy Spirit in us; it renders our bond with the Church more perfect; it gives us a special strength of the Holy Spirit to spread and defend the faith

> by word and action as true witnesses of Christ, to confess the name of Christ boldly, and never to be ashamed of the Cross . . .[15]

The 'character', the indelible spiritual mark received in confirmation, 'perfects the common priesthood of the faithful . . . and "the confirmed person receives the power to profess faith in Christ publicly and as it were officially (*quasi ex officio*)" '.[16]

Confirmation – a question of age or time?

In 1975 the *Revised Rite of Confirmation* stated:

> With regard to children, in the Latin Church the administration of confirmation is generally delayed until about the seventh year. For pastoral reasons, however, especially to implant deeply in the lives of the faithful complete obedience to Christ the Lord and a firm witnessing to him, the conferences of bishops may set an age that seems more suitable. This means that the sacrament is given, after the formation proper to it, when the recipients are more mature.[17]

In 1972 the *Rite of Christian Initiation of Adults* (R.C.I.A.) was published and gradually became the norm for initiation in the Catholic Church. The pattern suggested by the R.C.I.A. reverted to the early Church practice of baptism, confirmation and Eucharist, a liturgical unity of three rites of initiation. It can be argued, therefore, that this pattern should be reflected throughout the Church, so that for adults and children the order for sacraments is baptism and confirmation before first communion. This might mean following the tradition of the Eastern Orthodox Church, where there is a unified celebration of baptism and confirmation. The R.C.I.A. states:

> In accord with the ancient practice followed in the Roman liturgy, adults are not to be baptised without receiving confirmation immediately afterward, unless some serious reason stands in the way. The conjunction of the two celebrations signifies the unity of the paschal mystery, the close

> link between the mission of the Son and the outpouring of the Holy Spirit, and the connection between the two sacraments through which the Son and the Holy Spirit come with the Father to those who are baptised.[18]

Applying this to infants, if it is right to baptise them it is right to confirm them, too. Confirmation would be the completion of baptism. The ordinary minister of confirmation would be the priest in a parish.

If the emphasis in confirmation is on mature commitment to the Church, then an argument for receiving the sacrament at a minimum age of 12 or 13 can be put forward. Here, those who were baptised as infants can make a more mature decision to be confirmed in Church. It is a sign of their own commitment, and is a chance for both the candidate and the parish to prepare for this important event. The bishop would remain the minister of confirmation, and his visit to a parish, it is argued, would be a sign to the candidate of the wider universal Church to which he/she is making a mature commitment.

A further suggestion stems from the R.C.I.A. where adults who are received into the Church are confirmed. This is a sign of their commitment to the life of the Church which they wish to serve in some way. It is argued that the same should apply to all the baptised. Someone who was baptised as an infant, therefore, might in early or late adulthood decide to serve the Church in some concrete way. Such an adult would present him/herself for confirmation by the bishop or parish priest as a sign of their commitment to service.

Other ideas might be put forward to aid reflection on the age and time of confirmation. It might be deemed right to maintain confirmation for adolescents, but, following examples in the Lutheran and Episcopalian churches, also introduce 'rites of affirmation' to be celebrated at appropriate times. Some Episcopalian churches celebrate such a rite before the bishop comes for confirmation of adolescents. At this rite, those who wish reaffirm their own baptismal commitment. Lutheran churches celebrate a similar rite for all church members when somebody joins the church.

REFLECTION

- The unity of baptism, confirmation and Eucharist was completely separated when, in 1910, Pope Pius X encouraged communion for children from the age of seven. What advantages can you think of in three separate stages of initiation? By being separated from baptism and Eucharist has the status of confirmation in fact been raised?
- There are a number of varying emphases concerning the meaning of confirmation today. If you have been confirmed, what emphasis were you given? If you haven't been confirmed, what is there in confirmation that appeals to you as a sacrament?
- Do you see confirmation as part of initiation or as a separate strengthening rite in itself?

Confirmation – a typical case?

In many Catholic parishes, the first stirrings of confirmation are probably determined by a letter from Bishop's House, notifying the parish priest of the date for 'Visitation & Confirmation' some 12–18 months hence. That letter will also indicate diocesan policy for confirmation (e.g. 'Candidates should be at least 11 years old').

Once again statistics, that strange bed-fellow of religion, suggest that nearly 300 young people a week stop going to church! (Of course, absence from church should not be equated with loss of faith). So, many of the young people aged 11+ might not be present at church services. How are they going to know about confirmation? I have come across a number of variations of what happens next: the parish priest goes to the local secondary school(s) and obtains the names and addresses of all potential confirmation candidates living in the parish; a letter is then sent to their parents to tell them when their child/children can be confirmed; or the priest writes to the candidates, telling them when the confirmation programme is starting and notifying them of the date for confirmation; or the priest puts a note about confirmation in the parish bulletin, inviting anyone who might like to think about confirmation to write back with a word or two of explanation.

Once there is a group of candidates (or even before) the priest might also form a group of catechists whose role will be to hand on faith, to prepare the candidates for confirmation. This formation for the candidates is now largely parish-based. There will be a Service of Enrolment at the start of the programme, a number of sessions with the candidates over a period of perhaps six months, involvement of the parish through prayer partners, service projects, and other initiatives, and there will be a retreat/day of recollection for the candidates shortly before confirmation, and then the day itself: 'Be sealed with the gift of the Holy Spirit.'

Such a scenario raises a number of practical questions when it is put up against the theology of confirmation as seen before. If confirmation is an opportunity for the individual to make a personal commitment, is there a chance that pressure might be brought to bear upon candidates to make such a commitment (by either parents or peer pressure), so that those unable to do so would be left thinking they were 'second class citizens'? Confirmation in such a case would not be the total, mature commitment envisaged by the sacrament. Typical answers to 'Why do you want to be confirmed?' might be: 'It wasn't my decision, my gran wants it done', or 'Everybody in the class is being done, so I'm not going to be the odd one out.' If we claim that the sacrament of confirmation needs a measure of commitment and response on the part of the recipient, then we need to make sure that candidates are not confirmed without question but that they take the sacrament seriously.

Furthermore, if the sacrament is all about commitment is it in fact in danger of becoming a celebration of the candidate, rather than a celebration of what God does for us? If the emphasis is on maturity, is this at the expense of emphasising the power of God? While it is true that sacraments demand a response, the heart of every sacrament is God's gift of himself to the individual through Christ. In confirmation we are celebrating the completion of our identification with Christ, and the ability to respond is in itself God's gift. At the outset, confirmation was seen as part of a process of initiation; does commitment in some way mark the end of a process, is it seen as an 'achievement', so that once someone is 'done' there is no need for further Christian education and development?

Other practical, pastoral and educational problems arise. If confirmation is for those aged at least 11, then you might have a group of candidates ranging from 11 to 17. Are all these making the same mature commitment to their faith and their church? And what if there are adults within the parish who are to be confirmed, too? (Or what if an adult is to be baptised and confirmed as part of initiation at the Easter Vigil. That adult is not 'confirming' baptismal promises as if they were an event in the past. The adolescent receives the same sacrament, maybe 12 or 13 years after baptism. Is the adolescent doing what the adult is not doing?) As regards the preparation itself, how much emphasis is to be put on what the individual 'knows', rather than on his/her personal commitment to Jesus Christ and how that might be lived out in the local community?

One reaction to some of these pastoral and educational problems might be to delay confirmation, so that it is celebrated in early adulthood, or to return confirmation to its original position immediately after baptism. But then if we believe that sacraments mark important stages of life, are we left with a situation where the important years of adolescence are in no way marked or celebrated in terms of faith and church? Would there be no 'strengthening' for young people during those important years?

However, one of the dangers of such an approach is to see sacraments as 'one-off' events. If the first stirrings of confirmation stem from a letter giving a date, then the danger is that preparation might focus on that one date. It is interesting that recent sacramental programmes for confirmation offer pre- and post-confirmation work, so that the sacrament is not an isolated event for young people:

> . . . it should be the aim of every Confirmation programme to get across [the fact that the message of Jesus is relevant today]. One way of achieving this is to plant the Christian message within the sphere of the young person's present experience and let it grow . . . Understanding about life

> is more than knowing how the human body functions. Likewise, understanding about Confirmation is more than knowing only about the 'mechanics' of the sacrament . . . For these reasons, the programme aims to be more a faith programme than solely a Confirmation programme.[19]

Confirmation – a final comment

In 1985, in a Letter to the Youth of the World, John Paul II called on the Church to 're-think – and very profoundly – the meaning of baptism and confirmation . . . From these there begins the path towards the Eucharist'. This reflected the 1971 Introduction to the *Rite of Confirmation*, which began: 'Those who have been baptised continue on the path of Christian initiation through the sacrament of confirmation.'[20] Later on it is stated:

> Confirmation takes place as a rule within Mass in order that the fundamental connection of this sacrament with all of Christian initiation may stand out in clearer light. Christian initiation reaches its culmination in the communion of the body and blood of Christ. The newly confirmed therefore participate in the Eucharist, which completes their Christian initiation.[21]

Confirmation is a sacrament of initiation before it is a sacrament of commitment or maturity.

REFLECTION

- In terms of confirmation should we be talking about the right 'age' or the right 'time'?
- Candidates for confirmation are required to have a sponsor. The 1983 *Code of Canon Law* states that their function is 'to take care that the person confirmed behaves as a true witness of Christ and faithfully fulfils the duties inherent in this sacrament'.[22] How realistic is this for sponsoring 11–17 year olds or adults? If you have been a sponsor, what did you do? What would you request of a sponsor? The *Cat-*

echism of the Catholic Church adds that to emphasise the unity of baptism and confirmation one of the sponsors should 'be one of the baptismal godparents'.[23] What difference do you think this will make?

- Are there any comments you would make about the confirmation scenario painted above? Is it faithful to a theology of the sacrament?
- One idea is to celebrate infant baptism, followed by celebration of confirmation at seven years and First Communion at eight. The first celebration of reconciliation would come at a time appropriate to the child. Other liturgies would mark various stages of a child's life (e.g. transition from primary to secondary school). What comments would you make?

Confirmation is the moment
in which you complete
what the teachers of long ago used to call
your journey of Christian initiation:
The gift of the Spirit
makes you a living stone
in that dwelling place of God
amidst humanity that we call the Church.
The Church counts on you for its existence:
Even though you are young,
you're able and ready to become, like Jesus,
one who serves.
You will receive a gift, but it's a heavy gift;
I'd call it a seed that can bear wonderful fruit.

(Carlo Maria Martini,
Letter to a boy preparing for Confirmation)[24]

5 Eucharist

'Rite of passage that commands a high price' said the headline in *The Independent*. The article was about what it called the 'annual First Communion season', resulting in dresses for the girls that cost as much as £150 and which will only be worn once. As a student-priest in Rome I spent Sundays helping in a parish on the outskirts of the city. The 'First Communion season' went on for some time, and there were so many children receiving their First Communion that it took a month of 9.00 a.m. special Masses on Sunday to fit them all in. In fact, if you weren't related to anyone making their First Communion you weren't allowed to go to that Mass, you had to attend Mass in the parish hall. The parish priest would only allow one video-camera (from which you could then buy the 'official' video), and parents and relations would compete to buy their child/relation the best present – it was common, ten years ago, for a child to receive two computers for his/her First Communion. And after the religious ceremonies, the family and relations would go on to an expensive restaurant in the hills or by the sea that they had booked for the day. And I thought I was doing well with a boiled egg and jelly and ice-cream!

First Communion is still built up as an exciting day in a child's religious life, an unforgettable moment (although I remember one parent telling me he was deeply disappointed when he made his First Communion, because the host 'had no sherbet in it'! They'd obviously been rehearsing with 'Flying Saucer' sweets!). It's importance is hinted at in a popular baptismal course used in many parishes which takes parents through four stages in the Rite of Baptism. It suggests that the Rite should be begin at the door of the church, where everybody is welcomed; it proceeds to a lectern, from where the Word of God is proclaimed; from there to the font, where the baptism itself takes place; and finally the Rite is concluded at the altar rails or the altar, because that is where the parents 'will eventually be leading their child – to First Communion and the weekly Eucharist.'[1]

But what exactly is this sacrament which is seen as the focal point of the life of faith and whose first reception is so memorable for many generations of people?

Origins

I wonder how many of us were taught in school or left with the impression that the 'Last Supper' was the 'First Mass'? For me, that conjures up a bizarre image of Jesus in his vestments, surrounded by the twelve. Were they altar servers or congregation? Or were they concelebrating? Was there a hymn at the beginning, one at the Offertory Procession, and a 'Communion Hymn'?

We know, of course, that this was not the case. What we now call the Last Supper was a unique meal, recalling the Passover meal which celebrated how the people of Israel were saved, how their new life began. It was not simply a Passover meal. John's gospel tells us that during the meal Jesus got up from table, 'removed his outer garment and, taking a towel, wrapped it round his waist; he then poured water into a basin and began to wash his disciples' feet and to wipe them with the towel he was wearing' (John 13:4–5). He broke the bread used in the meal, gave it to his companions, and said 'This is my body'; and with the cup he said 'This is my blood, the blood of the new covenant', and gave it to them to drink.

But our oldest account of what happened at this meal is contained in Paul's first letter to the people of Corinth, written about AD 57; Paul says:

> For this is what I received from the Lord, and in turn passed on to you: that on the same night that he was betrayed, the Lord Jesus took some bread, and thanked God for it and broke it, and he said, 'This is my body,

> which is for you; do this as a memorial of me'. In the same way he took the cup after supper, and said, 'This cup is the new covenant in my blood. Whenever you drink it, do this as a memorial of me'. (1 Cor. 11:23–5)

Paul is writing to people who have begun to abuse what was obviously an established meal in the early Christian communities ('They went as a body to the Temple every day but met in their houses for the breaking of bread' Acts 2:46). They are not, Paul says, eating 'the Lord's Supper, since when the time comes to eat, everyone is in such a hurry to start his own supper that one person goes hungry while another is getting drunk' (1 Cor. 11:20–21). To correct such abuses, Paul reminds the people of Corinth of the origins of what they should be doing. He reminds them of the unity of the celebration: 'The blessing-cup that we bless is a communion with the blood of Christ, and the bread that we break is a communion with the body of Christ. The fact there is only one loaf means that, though there are many of us, we form a single body because we all share in this one loaf' (1 Cor. 10:16–18); 'Until the Lord comes, therefore, every time you eat this bread and drink this cup, you are proclaiming his death, and so anyone who eats the bread or drinks the cup of the Lord unworthily will be behaving unworthily towards the body and blood of the Lord' (11:26–7); and so, 'Whatever you eat, whatever you drink, whatever you do at all, do it for the glory of God' (10:31).

The phrase 'Institution of the Eucharist' refers to the specific texts in the gospels, written later than Paul's letter, recounting what happened at the Last Supper. Matthew, Mark and Luke simply relate Jesus' words at the meal, while John omits the words and tells the story of Jesus washing his disciples' feet (John 13). Teaching on the Eucharist is to be found in John 6, where Jesus declares:

> I am the bread of life. Your fathers ate the manna in the desert and they are dead; but this is the bread that comes down from heaven, so that a man may eat it and not die. I am the living bread which has come down from heaven. Anyone who eats this bread will live for ever; and the bread that I shall give is my flesh, for the life of the world . . .

> For my flesh is real food and my blood is real drink. He who eats my flesh and drinks my blood lives in me and I live in him. (6:48–51, 55–6)

It would seem that this text, written possibly around AD 90, is a clear indication that the Christian community believed Christ to be present in the bread and wine at their ritual meal. It was a simple celebration, with the 'breaking of bread' taking place during the meal. The importance of this fact cannot be overlooked.

The early Christians continued to meet after the death and resurrection of Jesus. At the Last Supper he had said 'Do this in memory of me' and his followers believed he was present in the bread and wine used at the fellowship meal. Paul's great emphasis on the unity of the meal would seem to suggest that fellowship of those around the table was a strong theme of Eucharist in the early Church.

The notion of a fellowship meal is an important religious theme, often linked with sacrificial elements. It was believed that a meal would increase the unity among those present, and so in many cultures it would be a grave insult to turn down an invitation to a meal. It would be interpreted as saying 'I have nothing to do with you'. In tribal religions, a meal was also a sign of the link between the participants and their god. It is clear that in the early Church Christ's continued presence was celebrated at a fellowship meal, where the Christians responded to Christ's request to 'Do this in memory of me'. It was a sign of the unity of believers and of the presence of Christ among them.

REFLECTION

- What are your first memories of Mass? Were you taught about the Last Supper in terms of the 'first Mass'?
- Think of any recent celebration (e.g. birthday, anniversary) you have attended. What made it 'good' and enjoyable? What elements contributed to the atmosphere and enjoyment?

- Think of a recent celebration of Mass that you enjoyed. What elements contributed to the joyful nature of the celebration?
- For the first Christians it was important to gather at a fellowship meal. Do our liturgical celebrations today have any indications that we are celebrating a fellowship meal? Have we lost or gained anything?

Ritual

The 'breaking of bread' was the focus of early Christian worship. For very practical reasons – because congregations increased in size and the meal was open to the kinds of abuse seen in Corinth – it seems that the communal meal disappeared. The celebration was also transferred from the Jewish Sabbath to Sunday, the first day of the week (cf. Acts 20:7), since it was on this day that Jesus rose from the dead. The language of the meal also changed, as it was taken for granted that you used your own language at the celebration. Jesus would have spoken Aramaic, but Greek-speaking Christians in the early Church would have spoken Greek (an obvious point, but an interesting one in view of the ever-continuing debate on language in the liturgy). To the people of Corinth Paul said: 'I thank God that I have a greater gift of tongues than all of you, but when I am in the presence of the community I would rather say five words that mean something than ten thousand words in a tongue' (1 Cor. 14:18–19). The language used in the celebration had to be understood by everybody.

Gradually, the simple meal was replaced by a formal celebration sometimes termed *eucharist*, a Greek word meaning 'thanksgiving', since many of the prayers used in the celebration were of praise and thanksgiving to God. The two-part structure, taken from Jewish synagogue services, remained. The synagogue services began with readings from the Law and the Prophets, followed by a commentary, and so the Christians began their services with this biblical element, adding their own testimonies and stories of Jesus. The commentary on these eventually became the homily, or sermon. The second part of the service was the prayer of thanksgiving to

God, the remembrance of the events of the Last Supper, and communion. Fellowship meals had disappeared completely.

Evidence as to how the celebration developed is provided by a number of texts from the second century, a time of persecution for the Church. One of the earliest texts from this period is the *Didache*, a manual for missionaries who instructed communities in Syria. This document contains a eucharistic prayer without Jesus' words over the bread and wine (the 'words of institution'). One possible explanation for their absence is that the central mysteries of the faith were kept secret from those who had not yet been baptised, and so the words were not recorded in the text.

A more detailed description of Christian Eucharist is found in the work of St Justin, martyred in the middle of the second century. He wrote a defence of Christian practices (*Apologia*) to the Emperor. Justin provides a description of the weekly celebration, which takes place 'on the day called Sunday'. Everybody gathers together:

> and the memoirs of the apostles or the writings of the prophets are read, as long as time permits; then, when the reader has ceased, the president verbally instructs, and exhorts to the imitation of these good things. Then we all rise together and pray, and, as we before said, when our prayer is ended, bread and wine and water are brought, and the president in like manner offers prayers and thanksgivings, according to his ability, and the people assent, saying Amen; and there is a distribution to each, and a participation of that over which thanks have been given, and to those who are absent a portion is sent by the deacons. And they who are well to do, and willing, give what each thinks fit; and what is collected is deposited with the president, who succours the orphans and widows, and those who, through sickness or any other cause are in want . . .[2]

From Justin's writings certain elements in the Eucharist are clear: there is a liturgy of the Word and a eucharistic liturgy, an offertory, a eucharistic prayer (although it would seem there are no set prayers), communion, and a collection (one tradition that has remained steadfastly unchanged through the centuries!).

A more detailed description of the eucharistic celebration is contained in *The Apostolic Tradition*, written by Hippolytus, a Roman priest, about the year 215. There are two accounts of the celebration of the Eucharist, one at the rite of ordination for a bishop and one at the rite of baptism. In the first account, Hippolytus provides the first detailed eucharistic prayer we possess, a sign that by the start of the third century there were set prayer formulae (and this prayer is found in today's Missal as Eucharistic Prayer Two). The order of service is, in essence, the same as that provided by Justin. However, at the offertory many gifts are brought, not just bread and wine. These latter are presented to the bishop, while the rest of the gifts are put to one side. They would be given to the poor (although the system was gradually abused, with the clergy taking the best for themselves). The bishop pronounces the eucharistic prayer over the bread and wine, including an 'institution narrative'. The bread is broken and distributed and the consecrated wine is given to everyone. People received communion standing and took the consecrated bread in their hands and drank from the chalice.

Hippolytus stresses the importance of the Eucharist, speaking of it in reverential tones. He encourages people to receive communion before any other food, and nothing should be dropped or spilt. The practice of taking the Eucharist home for daily communion continued, although Hippolytus warned the people not to leave the sacred bread lying around the house where an unbaptised person, or even a mouse, might accidentally eat it!

By the third century, ritual had completely replaced the informality of the fellowship meal. The leader of the community presided, but it was very much the worship of the community gathered around their spiritual leader. 'It was a sacramental experience of communal worship offered in the presence of Christ, who became present as the community prayed and worshipped together. And what made the bread and wine sacred was the entire ritual action which repeated and commemorated what Christ had done at his Last Supper.'[3]

As the ritual became more formal, many of the early Christian writers began to develop one of the most important ideas associated with the Eucharist, that of sacrifice. In itself, sacrifice was a notion common among most religions. It was seen as a sign of dependence on gods and would be offered for many reasons: to influence them, to obey their will, or, more commonly, to maintain or restore a particular relationship. The Old Testament has many examples, one of the more memorable being the ratification of the covenant with Yahweh. The people of Israel had agreed to observe the commands of Yahweh, and so an altar was built at the foot of Mount Sinai. Moses then

> directed certain young Israelites to offer holocausts and to immolate bullocks to Yahweh as communion sacrifices. Half of the blood Moses took up and put into basins, the other half he cast on the altar. And taking the Book of the Covenant he read it to the listening people, and they said, 'We will observe all that Yahweh has decreed; we will obey.' Then Moses took the blood and cast it towards the people. 'This' he said 'is the blood of the Covenant that Yahweh has made with you . . .' (Exodus 24:5–8)

Another dramatic sacrifice was a sin offering, which symbolised the disobedience of the people and the transferring of those sins onto an animal which was then sacrificed to appease the god, cancel the sins, and be a sign of new life. Leviticus 16 describes the sin offering made on the Day of Atonement:

> [Aaron] must then immolate the goat for the sacrifice for the sin of the people, and take its blood through the veil. With this blood he is to do as with the blood of the bull, sprinkling it on the throne of mercy and in front of it. This is how he is to perform the rite of atonement over the sanctuary for the uncleanness of the sons of Israel, for their transgressions and for all their sins. (Lev. 16:15–16).

The ideas of ritual meal and sacrifice received their greatest expression in *the* ritual meal of the Israelites, the Passover. This meal recalled how Yahweh passed over the doors of the Israelites and slew the first-born Egyptians and how the Israelites then passed dry-shod over the Red Sea (Exodus 12, 14). The

Israelites had sacrificed a lamb and sprinkled the door-posts with its blood to protect them from death; their meal then had to be prepared with unleavened bread and eaten in haste so that they could leave Egypt. Every year this meal is celebrated by Jews, and in the gospels we occasionally come across the phrase 'it was about the time of the Passover', showing that it was an important part of Jewish life at the time of Christ. The meal is, in many respects, sacramental, for it re-enacts the events it commemorates in such a way that they become real to all who celebrate the Passover.

In the pagan world of the first few centuries after Christ's death, Christians were criticised for not offering sacrifices to gods. Justin, in his *Apologia* in defence of Christianity, said that Christians celebrated a true sacrifice. He called the Eucharist the 'sacrifice of the Church', while Irenaeus (*c.* 200) said Christians offered a new covenant sacrifice to God. In the minds of early Christian writers, participation in a fellowship meal had been replaced by the idea of being united with Christ's offering of himself to the Father. Eucharist was participation in Christ's sacrifice.

Some of the early Christians would have been aware of the gospel accounts of the Last Supper, where Jesus spoke of his blood as 'the blood of the covenant poured out for many for the forgiveness of sins' (Matt. 26:28). Irenaeus stressed this in declaring: 'The Eucharist is the flesh and blood of our saviour, the flesh which suffered for our sins and which the Father raised from the dead.'[4] Justin expressed the Christian belief that 'the food which has been made Eucharist through the prayer formed out of the words of Christ, and which nourishes and becomes our flesh and blood, is the flesh and blood of the same Jesus who was made incarnate.'[5]

From Eucharist to liturgy

In 313, Emperor Constantine lifted the ban on Christian worship. In 380, Theodosius proclaimed Christianity to be the state religion of the Roman Empire. Significantly, the Eucharist became not just a religious ritual but also a state function. It was becoming less and less a fellowship meal, but more an elaborate, complicated ritual ceremony.

This was reflected not only in how the ceremony developed, but even in its name. The fellowship meal of the 'Lord's Supper' had been the 'Eucharist' (thanksgiving); that now became the *liturgy*, from a Greek word meaning a 'public work' or a 'service in the name of/on behalf of the people'. This was a significant change. It suggested that people had become on-lookers rather than participants, as a bishop or priest performed a service of worship for them.

Although the standard structure of the ceremony remained the same (an offering of the gifts of bread and wine, a prayer of thanksgiving recalling the Last Supper, and distribution of communion), additional prayers were added by bishops and priests and some important formal aspects crept into the celebration. In the past, the leader of the community had no set 'vestments' for the meal, although it was presumed he would wear his best clothing. But Constantine had given bishops a rank as judges in the state system, and so they had to have signs of rank – a cape, headgear, and a ring – which they had to wear at public functions. And since judges sat on a throne, were accompanied by incense and torch-bearers, and had people genuflect to them as a sign of respect, these elements of ceremonial were introduced to the liturgy. It would seem that priests were not accorded such honours! In fact, even in the fifth century Pope Celestine I was quite horrified by the way such elegant dressing was detracting from the celebration, and he wrote: 'We must distinguish ourselves from the people by doctrine, not by vestment; by manners, not by habit; by purity of spirit, not by adornment . . . We must instruct and not deceive. It is not a matter of inspiring the eyes, but of teaching souls.'[6]

As congregations increased, special buildings were needed in which to celebrate, and Constantine gave the Christians many buildings for worship. He also built special halls for this purpose, modelling them on state buildings, rectangular in shape with a raised platform at one end. These buildings were termed 'royal' in Greek – *basilicoi*, hence 'basilica', and significantly they were designed for watching rather than participating.

More important changes in the liturgy were stimulated by theology. At the start of the fourth century an African named Arius declared that Christ was not God. He believed that Jesus was just an ordinary human being and not divine. Arianism, as it came to be known, was condemned at the Council of Nicaea in 325, which declared that Jesus was 'one in being' with the Father. The effect on the liturgy was dramatic. Christians believed that Jesus was made present in the changing of the bread and wine; and since Jesus was identified with God people felt themselves unworthy to receive communion and come into contact with God. Thus, there was a steady decline in numbers receiving communion. The prevailing attitude was perfectly described by Cyril of Jerusalem in his catechetical lectures in the middle of the fourth century. He emphasised awe and reverence, and spoke of Jesus' presence in the Eucharist as 'that most terrifying hour'! He gave detailed instructions on how to receive communion, ensuring that people used their left hand 'as a throne for the right hand which must receive the King'. Cyril often refers to the 'fearful' presence in the Eucharist and such sentiments discouraged people from receiving communion. John Chrysostom (*c.* 347–407) even spoke of the table of the Lord as a place of 'terror and shuddering'.

Gradually, the language of the liturgy also changed. In Rome, the language of the common people – a 'vulgar' language – was Latin. Pope Callistus (*c.* 217–222), who himself had been a slave, had stated as early as the third century that the liturgy should be in the language of the people – Latin. Towards the end of the fourth century Latin was used more and more, and the liturgy became known as the *missarum solemnia*, a 'ceremony of dismissals' (referring to those undergoing instruction who were dismissed after the sermon and the entire congregation dismissed after communion). Technically, *missa* referred to the dismissal of soldiers. By 400, the term was applied to any act of public worship, and by 800 it became an exclusive term for Christian worship, because of the final phrase of the 'mass': *Ite missa est* – 'Go, the Mass is ended'.

REFLECTION

- 'Fellowship meal' – 'Eucharist' – 'liturgy' – 'Mass': with each name-change there seems a shift in emphasis in the nature of the celebration. Is there any emphasis which particularly appeals to you? For what reasons?
- 'The sacrifice of the Mass' is a phrase still in current usage. In what ways do you see the Mass as a sacrifice? How important is it today to remember that the Mass is a sacrifice?
- 'Liturgy' is a service in the name of/on behalf of the people. How true do you think this is of any liturgical celebrations you have attended or heard about?
- Under the Emperor Constantine, places of worship were purpose-built, and these gradually became more grandiose as the liturgy became more formalised. Mosaics, gilded ceilings, marble altars replacing wooden tables, jewelled crosses, silver and gold vessels – what do you think such symbols were trying to convey about the liturgy? How important are symbols today?

The 'Golden Age'

'The good old days' is a phrase often used today in many contexts. For some, I am sure, such a phrase would be applied to what they might see as the 'good old days' of Latin Mass. This implies a time when everything was almost perfect, a 'Golden Age'. Of course, no such perfect or 'golden' age ever existed or ever will. But as almost a technical term the time between the so-called Peace of Constantine in 313 and the death of Pope St Gregory the Great in 604 is often referred to as the 'Golden Age' of the eucharistic liturgy.

Increasingly, both prayers and directions as to how to celebrate were written down. In this way the celebration became less of a spontaneous event and more of an organised ritual. Order and precision were the key characteristics, with precise roles assigned to both celebrant and congregation. The *Gregorian Sacramentary* is the name given to a number of books traditionally, though mistakenly, ascribed to Pope St Gregory the Great (590–604) and the forerunner of today's *Roman Missal*. An example of the change in the language of the liturgy in the *Gregorian Sacramentary* is interesting. What today we call the Eucharistic Prayer is referred to as the 'Canon', the 'rule'. This implies a prayer that the celebrant was obliged to say without changing anything – a far remove from the spontaneous prayers of earlier gatherings.

The *Gregorian Sacramentary* provides a detailed account of a Papal Mass around the year 600. Without going into the minute details of such a Mass, there are many recognisable elements in the set structure of the celebration: a solemn entry, the singing of the *kyrie eleison* (with the *Gloria* sung on feast days), readings, an offertory, the Preface, the *Sanctus*, and the Canon. This, and the words of the consecration, are recited in a low voice heard only by those close to the pope. The consecrated bread and chalice are not raised until the end of the Canon, which was followed by the *Pater noster* (Our Father). For communion, the pope receives first; then the announcements are made and those not receiving communion leave. After the people have received communion, there is a final prayer at the altar and the dismissal, *Ite, missa est*.

This simple outline bears much resemblance to the celebration of Mass today. To some extent, it was a mixture of religious symbolism and the trappings of court officialdom. In terms of the development of the celebration, there was now a fixed, central part of the Mass (the Canon); a set language – Latin – was used, and there was a series of plainsong chants to accompany a rich ceremonial. However, the emphasis was clearly on the clergy, who dominated the liturgy. The role of lay people was limited to responding to the prayers, bringing their gifts to the altar, and receiving communion. It is perhaps ironic that liturgy in its 'Golden Age' was, for the majority of the congregation, something they watched and attended rather than took part in. The rich ceremonial, with processions and all the trappings thereof, made the liturgy a wonderful spectacle to watch, rather than a special meal to share in.

However, the elaborate ceremonial did have its purpose. Where it was successful was in emphasising the divine presence in the Eucharist. Many people began to see the liturgy as the presence of God himself and that presence was related specifically to the eucharistic prayer. Here again is an important sacramental development: whereas in the past there had been a general feeling of the presence of Christ in the fellowship meal, many church writers now began to focus on the moment when Christ became truly present – at the moment when the Last Supper was remembered and the words of institution were repeated. Ambrose of Milan, towards the end of the fourth century, said: 'This bread was in fact bread before the sacramental words were spoken, but at the moment of consecration it becomes the flesh of Christ . . . It is . . . the words of Christ which produce this sacrament, words such as those through which he created all things.'[7]

The emphasis on the presence of God had, as seen before, contributed to a gradual decline in the numbers receiving communion. This was also linked to the notion of sacrifice, for the Eucharist came to be seen as a sacrifice that could be offered to God without everybody fully participating. The sacrifice was offered on behalf of the people by the bishop or priest; that sacrifice was Christ, offered by the Church to God. People participated in the sacrifice by uniting themselves with Christ on the altar, by uniting themselves with his sacrifice, and thereby they became one with God and with each other. Such were the profound reflections of church writers at the time; the reality for a large number of people was that liturgy had become a public function which they attended, rather than a celebration of their faith through worship.

The privatisation of the Mass

Moving into the Middle Ages, one of the most important changes in the development of the Mass was the shift from the community to the individual, from a meal to a sacred action, from Sunday public worship to weekday private Masses. It is perhaps ironic that one of the reasons for this lies in the increased emphasis on the Mass as sacrifice, for if it was so then the Mass could be offered for a number of reasons whenever necessary – for a good harvest, for good health, for all sorts of things. And in very practical terms, there was the problem of many priests gathering around the same altar – increasingly, those who wanted to celebrate privately did so, at their own altar, often with nobody else present.

This was far removed from the pomp and ceremonial of the 'Golden Age' of liturgy, and such Masses – with little or no congregation – became the norm in Europe and were known as 'low' Masses. In a sense there were now two types of worship: public, on Sundays, and private, on weekdays. With private Masses there came the growth of 'intentions' at Mass. Originally, those who had asked for a specific intention would provide the offertory gifts, and these Masses became known as 'votive' Masses, i.e. offered for a specific intention for a suitable donation. The most popular of intentions were for the deceased, and weekday votive Masses became almost exclusively Masses for the deceased.

These Masses were said in Latin, a language understood only by the clergy, and so once again the notion of a congregation watching the spectacle unfold before them was reinforced. People attended a spectacle, they did not really participate in a liturgy. This was even reflected in the solemn Sunday liturgies, where the celebrant's actions became more and more complicated. For example, the celebrant would read the epistle at the right side of the altar and the gospel at the left. The allegorical explanation, aside from the practical idea of letting people know where they were up to in the Latin liturgy, was simple: in the Old Testament, God spoke to the just (on the right), but now in the New Testament he speaks even to sinners (on the left).

As the number of people receiving communion continued to decline, emphasis shifted to adoration and contemplation of the real presence of Christ in the consecrated host. It was a shift towards piety rather than participation; people were made aware of their unworthiness to receive the body and blood of Christ and so they preferred to express their faith by contemplating the consecrated host rather than receiving it.

Seeing the consecrated host became the high-point of Mass. For people to see the host, the priest had to elevate it and this became the norm. Sadly, superstition crept in and there arose a belief that seeing the consecrated host guaranteed that a person would not die suddenly that day. People would go from church to church to see the host as often as possible, and would find the places in church with the best view. There are even accounts, in England, of people crying out to the celebrant 'Higher, Sir John, higher!' when the host was not raised high enough.[8] Since the Mass was in Latin, a bell would be rung so that people would know when to look up to see the host. Devotion and piety had completely replaced participation (a move that would gradually lead to the popularity of Blessed Sacrament processions, thereby offering further opportunities to see the consecrated host contained in the monstrance – from the Latin verb *monstrare*, to show). For those who did receive communion, changes which crept in from the ninth century onwards reflected further aspects of the unworthiness of receiving. People were warned not to touch the body of Christ, and so communion was given on the tongue, no longer in the hands. It was easier to receive communion in this way if the communicant was kneeling down – also a further sign of respect. And to enable people to kneel, an arm rest was provided – the communion rail. Since the numbers receiving were so small, a loaf of bread was no longer needed for mass, and so small, white wafers were introduced – these were called *hosts*, from a Latin word for a sacrificial victim.

Such changes were reflected in the lay-out of churches. The altar was placed against the rear wall, with the priest facing east with his back to the people. It was no longer a celebration of priest and people gathered around the altar, but a celebration by the priest, watched by the people who could observe various gestures from a distance. It was a sacrifice, not a service of communion and thanksgiving; it was offered by the priest alone, for the people, in a language the people did not understand, and largely in silence anyway. The distance between the altar and the people gradually increased, with various 'obstacles' separating the two: communion rails, benches for the choir, statues, arches, and so on. The people were now completely cut off from the celebration of Mass. Participation had been replaced by adoration or just observing what went on. With the introduction of more and more choral music, people actually got into the habit of going to 'hear' Mass. By 1215, participation in the Mass had reached such a low that the Fourth Lateran Council felt it necessary to decree that people had to receive communion 'at least once a year'. The Mass had become a clerical domain, a mystery which people did not understand but were encouraged to watch.

REFLECTION

- As the liturgy became more elaborate, the emphasis shifted to focusing on the divine presence. How do you think this was achieved and what were its advantages?
- The entire liturgy became surrounded with an aura of mystery, something that the people believed but could not understand. How important do you think this aspect of 'mystery' is?
- Private, or 'votive' Masses became the norm. Can the Mass ever be 'private'?
- The tradition of adoration of the consecrated host (the Blessed Sacrament) is one that has remained strong down to the present day. What do you think is its importance today?

Transubstantiation

Gradually, the celebration of the Eucharist became more rigid, more uniform throughout the Christian world. Although some localised rites still existed, there was, on the whole, a recognised model of celebration. One of the effects of this was that in the Middle Ages the focus shifted from the Mass to the sacrament, from the 'how' of celebration to the very nature of that celebration.

For scholastic theologians of the thirteenth century one of the most important questions they tackled was *the* central question: how were the bread and wine changed into the body and blood of Christ? The answer has remained unchanged down the centuries, and is expressed in today's *Catechism of the Catholic Church* in this way:

> The Council of Trent summarises the Catholic faith by declaring: 'Because Christ our Redeemer said that it was truly his body that he was offering under the species of bread, it has always been the conviction of the Church of God . . . that by the consecration of the bread and wine there takes place a change of the whole substance of the bread into the substance of the body of Christ our Lord and of the whole substance of the wine into the substance of his blood. This change the holy Catholic Church has fittingly and properly called *transubstantiation*.'[9]

The term 'transubstantiation' was first used by Hildebert of Tours (1056–1133). Nearly one hundred years later, Pope Innocent III, in a letter to the Archbishop of Lyons, referred to the words 'used by Christ Himself when He transubstantiated (*transubstantiavit*) the bread and wine into His body and blood'.[10] In 1215 the Fourth Lateran General Council used the term 'transubstantiation' in an official church document for the first time. But what was the reality expressed by this new word?

In simple terms, transubstantiation meant that the reality or substance of the bread and wine changed, even though they still looked like bread and wine. The scholastic theologians used many complicated philosophical notions to describe this change. The 'substance' of something was its permanent, underlying reality; this contrasted with the changing nature of its visible 'accidents' (or appearance, e.g. colour, shape, etc.). In the Eucharist, at the words of consecration, the substance of the bread and wine changed, its reality changed into the reality of Christ's body and blood. But the accidents remained the same – visibly the elements were the same. This was such a unique change that it required a unique terminology – hence, transubstantiation. In this sacrament, then, God was offering union with Christ through communion.

One of the great theologians of this time, St Thomas Aquinas, said that the physical make-up of the bread and wine pointed to something else, was a sign of something else; in this sense, the bread and wine signified, pointed to the body and blood of Christ. And so the sacrament was being united with Christ, present in the Eucharist in his body and blood. Aquinas also pointed out an important, but perhaps 'automatic' element to the Eucharist, by emphasising that the priest's ability to consecrate the bread and wine came not from personal merit or worth but from the grace of ordination. This was the idea of *ex opere operato*, the emphasis on the work performed not the worker doing it.

However such theological reflections on the Eucharist did not increase participation. People were still reluctant to receive communion, and Mass gradually became a celebration dominated by the priest. Private Masses abounded, celebrated for particular intentions paid for by the people, and it was common to find several Masses going on at the same time at different altars in the one church.

This was the situation which greeted Martin Luther in the sixteenth century. He saw the way Mass was celebrated as superstition, and attacked the practice of Mass stipends and private Masses. But Luther did believe in the 'real presence' of Christ in the Eucharist and he explained it using the term 'consubstantiation'. This was the belief that bread and wine and Christ's body and blood were all present, co-existing in the Eucharist after the consecration. Other Protestant reformers disagreed with Luther. Calvin, for example, saw the bread and wine as a sign of Christ's body and blood. Significantly, there was not a *unified* Protestant position on the Eucharist.

The Council of Trent

In complete contrast, a strong unified Catholic position on the Eucharist was declared with great authority at the Council of Trent (1545–63). The Council's statements on the Eucharist were a response not only to the Protestant reformers, but also to the somewhat chaotic state of the liturgy within the Catholic Church itself. The bishops wanted to see a unified practice throughout the Church.

There were three important decrees in this regard: *Decree on the Most Holy Eucharist* (1551), *Doctrine on Communion under both species and on Communion of little children* (1562), and *Doctrine on the Most Holy Sacrifice of the Mass* (1562).

Already, the language used (e.g. 'Sacrifice of the Mass') suggests that the fellowship-meal idea of the Eucharist has been almost completely replaced by the notion of Eucharist as sacrifice:

> In this divine sacrifice which is celebrated in the Mass, the same Christ who offered Himself once in a bloody manner on the altar of the cross is contained and is offered in an unbloody manner. Therefore, the holy Council teaches that this sacrifice is truly propitiatory, so that, if we draw near to God with an upright heart and true faith, with fear and reverence, with sorrow and repentance, through it 'we may receive mercy and find grace to help in time of need' (cf. Heb. 4:16). For the Lord, appeased by this oblation, grants grace and the gift of repentance, and He pardons wrongdoings and sins, even grave ones. For, the victim is one and the same: the same now offers through the ministry of priests, who then offered Himself on the cross; only the manner of offering is different.[11]

The Council of Trent confirmed many of the beliefs of the Catholic Church that had been questioned in various ways by the Reformers: that after the consecration 'our Lord Jesus Christ, true God and man, is truly, really and substantially contained under the appearances of [bread and wine]';[12] this change is called transubstantiation; communion under both kinds is not necessary to receive Christ wholly, he is fully present equally in his body and his blood.

Clearly, a doctrinal foundation stone had been laid concerning the Church's ideas about the Eucharist. The liturgical practices of previous centuries, the theological debates of the Middle Ages, in a sense were summed up in Trent's profound yet precise statements. The clarity and uniformity were taken a stage further with the publication in 1570 of the *Roman Missal*. This text became mandatory for virtually the entire Catholic Church and could never be altered – on pain of excommunication! And so the Mass that my parents attended in the 1950s, nearly four hundred years later, was more or more less the celebration as decreed in the *Roman Missal* of Pope Pius V, dating from 1570. It was in Latin, the priest had his back to the people, many of whom were saying the Rosary as Mass went on. The choirs, increasingly popular over the centuries, added musical elements emphasising still more the notion of going to 'hear Mass' in churches ever more ornate in their architecture, painting, and decoration. Mass became a time for private prayer, with little or no connection even with receiving communion. It was as if three separate strands had developed in eucharistic sacramental doctrine: the sacrifice of the Mass, communion, and devotion to the Blessed Sacrament. What had begun as a celebration of Christ present among us had become a rigid liturgy with great emphasis on piety and devotion.

REFLECTION

- Is 'transubstantiation' a useful term in explaining Catholic belief in the Eucharist? Can you think of any other ways of describing the change of bread and wine?
- Some of the Reformers believed Christ was only present in the Eucharist 'in sign', a reminder of Christ's offering of his body and blood on the cross. In what ways might the Eucharist be more than just a sign, a pointer?
- The Council of Trent decreed that children did not need to receive communion until they had reached the age of reason – a child's spiritual needs came through baptism. Were they being denied something? What comments would you make concerning children and the spiritual benefits of receiving communion?
- The Council of Trent set the pattern for four hundred years of eucharistic celebration in the Catholic Church. What recollections or stories have you heard about Mass celebrated in this way? Can you think of advantages and disadvantages?

The Second Vatican Council

It might seem strange to jump straight from the Council of Trent, which closed in 1563, to the Second Vatican Council, which opened four hundred years later. But on the whole Catholic theology and practice concerning the sacrament of the Eucharist remained essentially unchanged throughout that time. The Council of Trent had become a definitive benchmark, with its emphasis on dogma and doctrine.

Gradually, however, there was a rediscovery of the idea of liturgy as public, community worship. What became known as the 'Liturgical Movement' received impetus from a number of Benedictine abbeys in the nineteenth century and had as its goal the restoration of active participation by the laity in the Church's public worship. Significant support for such an initiative came in 1905 when Pope Pius X encouraged people to receive communion on a regular basis and then again in 1910 when he decreed that children could receive communion once they had reached the age of reason. As we have seen, adults were in the habit of rarely going to communion (perhaps once a year) and children did not receive communion until they were 12 or even older. Henceforth, the celebration of 'First Communion' was to become more and more important.

In 1959, Pope John XXIII called an ecumenical council and the first document published by that council was the *Constitution on the Sacred Liturgy* (4 December 1963). The call for reform was echoed in the very first sentence: 'The sacred council has set out to impart an ever-increasing vigor to the Christian lives of the faithful; to adapt more closely to the needs of our age those institutions which are subject to change . . . Accordingly it sees particularly cogent reasons for undertaking the reform and promotion of the liturgy.'[13]

The new and key concept, repeated throughout the *Constitution*, is that of participation:

> It is very much the wish of the church that all the faithful should be led to take that full, conscious, and active part in liturgical celebrations which is demanded by the very nature of the liturgy, and to which the Christian people, 'a chosen race, a royal priesthood, a holy nation, a redeemed

> people' (1 Pet. 2:9, 4–5) have a right and to which they are bound by reason of their Baptism.[14]

The immediate practical steps aimed at facilitating such participation included Mass no longer being celebrated in Latin but in the 'vernacular' by a priest or number of priests who faced the people, who might have missals or leaflets to follow the readings and responses. (Today, lay participation is reflected in the ever greater ministries open to them, such as readers and extraordinary ministers of the Eucharist, to name but two.) What was once termed exclusively the 'holy sacrifice of the Mass' was now also referred to as a 'celebration of the Eucharist' by the priest *and* people, not just by the priest on behalf of the people:

> The church . . . spares no effort in trying to ensure that, when present at this mystery of faith, Christian believers should not be there as strangers or silent spectators. On the contrary, having a good grasp of it through the rites and prayers, they should take part in the sacred action, actively, fully aware, and devoutly. They should be formed by God's word, and be nourished at the table of the Lord's Body. They should give thanks to God. Offering the immaculate victim, not only through the hands of the priest but also together with him, they should learn to offer themselves.[15]

The *Constitution on the Sacred Liturgy* called for a richer use of Scripture, reintroduced the prayers of the faithful, and allowed communion under both kinds. Needless to say, change was painful. With hindsight, it might be true to say that change seemed to come about so quickly that some people found it difficult to cope with and still think back to the 'good old days'. But in terms of the theology of the Eucharist, the Second Vatican Council reinforced the centrality of this sacrament: 'From the liturgy . . . and especially from the Eucharist, grace is poured forth upon us as from a fountain, and our sanctification in Christ and the glorification of God to which all other activities of the Church are directed, as toward their end, are achieved with maximum effectiveness.'[16]

The close link between liturgy and the Eucharist meant that what developed from the Second Vatican Council was a theology of Eucharist as worship. This broad horizon replaced the previous narrow focus which tended to concentrate on the blessed sacrament or the consecration. Again, the stimulus for this was the *Constitution on the Sacred Liturgy.*

> At the Last Supper, on the night he was betrayed, our Saviour instituted the eucharistic sacrifice of his body and blood. This he did in order to perpetuate the sacrifice of the cross throughout the ages until he should come again, and so to entrust to his beloved spouse, the church, a memorial of his death and resurrection: a sacrament of love, a sign of unity, a bond of charity, 'a paschal banquet in which Christ is received, the mind is filled with grace, and a pledge of future glory is given to us'.[17]

Christ is truly present in the Church and in the Eucharist. The community gathers in worship to be nourished by the Word of God and the body of Christ. These are the emphases that form the heart of the sacrament of the Eucharist today. The *Catechism of the Catholic Church* states that in the Eucharist we receive the 'food that makes us live for ever in Jesus Christ'.[18] Furthermore, the Eucharist is not an end in itself for it must be a stimulus to action. It is a challenge for us not to be just 'Sunday Christians' but to acknowledge the unbreakable bond between faith and life:

> To receive in truth the Body and Blood of Christ given up for us, we must recognize Christ in the poorest, his brethren: 'You have tasted the Blood of the Lord, yet you do not recognize your brother . . . You dishonour this table when you do not judge worthy of sharing your food someone judged worthy to take part in this meal . . . God freed you from all your sins and invited you here, but you have not become more merciful.'[19]

There is a rediscovery of the fellowship meal first celebrated nearly two thousand years ago.

REFLECTION

- Active participation – what does this mean for you?
- How do you see the Eucharist as a celebration of both priest and people?
- 'It's boring' is a phrase still used today in relation to the Mass and yet most of the Mass changes every week. What might some people see as 'boring'?
- The two parts of the Mass – the Liturgy of the Word and the Liturgy of the Eucharist – are 'one single act of worship'.[20] Does this seem to be the case or do they seem like two different parts of Mass?
- We are nourished by the Word of God and fed by the Body of Christ. How does this affect daily life after Sunday?

The love of Christ
has drawn us here together.
In him,
let us exult and find our joy.
Although we are many
we form one body,
because we share in the one loaf.
The bread we break
is a communion in the body of Christ.
As this bread
was once scattered upon the mountains
and was gathered together and became one,
so let the Church be gathered
from the ends of the earth
into God's kingdom

(*The Sunday Missal*)[21]

6 *Reconciliation*

'Forgive Me Computer . . . For I Have Sinned', said the headline in a tabloid newspaper. The article described how it was now possible to confess your sins to a 'virtual priest' with the use of an 'electronic confessional' on a computer disc. The disc requires you to click on to the sins committed 'from a list of hundreds of evil deeds', and then the machine tells you what penance you have to perform to obtain forgiveness. Examples include 'one quick Hail Mary' for a white lie, while adultery 'will cost three Our Fathers and three Hail Marys'.

A similar story some years ago provoked the headline 'Computer Offers Forgiveness' and was written by a national newspaper's 'Technology Correspondent'. It seems as if confession – or reconciliation as it is now called – has moved with the times and entered the world of technology! Gone are the dark, sometimes dismal confessionals, replaced by the technology of the Automatic Confession Machine and the CD-ROM!

Of course, these stories are absurd. It is nonsense to suggest that a sacrament so rooted in Jesus's ministry of forgiveness could be reduced to pressing the right buttons and reading from a computer screen! The only true confession remains person-to-person with a priest. However, changes are afoot and the picture is changing. In many places it is no longer common to see row upon row of people waiting to 'go to confession' on Saturday, their numbers swelled at Christmas and Easter as people made their 'Easter duty'. It is a stark reality today that people no longer go to confession as often as in the past. Even our language has changed, as we now speak about the 'Sacrament of Reconciliation' rather than 'confession'. But is this just toying with language, making the sacrament sound less fearful when little else has changed?

The story is told of a priest showing a friend around the church, pointing out the altar, the baptismal font, the stations of the cross, and explaining the function and symbolism of all that surrounded him. 'This is marvellous,' his friend says. 'I didn't realise there was so much in a Catholic church. By the way, what is in there?' he asked, pointing to the door to the confessional. 'Oh nothing,' the priest replied, 'it's only the fire escape.'

Is that what the sacrament is about?

Forgiveness in the New Testament

One of the most memorable parables from the gospels is the one we call 'The Prodigal Son', found in Luke 15. The story is, of course, about God's constant love for sinners and is at the heart of Jesus' mission. His whole message was one of forgiveness and reconciliation, beginning with his call: 'The time has come and the kingdom of God is close at hand. Repent, and believe the Good News' (Mark 1:15). Jesus was criticised for associating with sinners, and when asked if we should forgive as often as seven times replied: 'Not seven, I tell you, but seventy-seven times' (Matt. 18:22). Clearly, Jesus' mission focused on reconciling people with God and with each other.

The early Christians believed that the role of reconciliation lay with the community in which the sinner acknowledged his/her sinfulness: 'If we say we have no sin in us, we are deceiving ourselves and refusing to admit the truth; but if we acknowledge our sins, then God who is faithful and just will forgive our sins and purify us from everything that is wrong. To say that we have never sinned is to call God a liar and to show that his word is not in us' (1 John 1:8–10). The important community role is emphasised by Paul, who writes to the people of Corinth expressing his displeasure that someone committing incest has not been expelled from the community: 'You must drive out this evil-doer from among you' (1 Cor. 5:13). But the community also had the authority to reinstate people, as Paul once again points out: 'The punishment already imposed by the majority on the man in question is enough;

and the best thing now is to give him your forgiveness and encouragement, or he might break down from so much misery' (2 Cor. 2:6–7).

This authority is reflected in the later gospel text where Jesus declares to Peter: 'I will give you the keys of the kingdom of heaven: whatever you bind on earth shall be considered bound in heaven; whatever you loose on earth shall be considered loosed in heaven' (Matt. 16:19). The power to 'bind and loose' signifies two things: to declare with authority that something is permitted or prohibited by divine law and to banish from or readmit to the community. The exclusion is to induce the sinner to repentance, recognised by readmittance to the community. In Matthew 18 this authority given to Peter is extended to the apostles (and thus to the Church).

John's gospel also provides an account of a resurrection appearance to the disciples where Jesus breathed on them and said: 'Receive the Holy Spirit. For those whose sins you forgive, they are forgiven; for those whose sins you retain, they are retained' (John 20:22–3). The Spirit confers to the Church, through the persons of the apostles and disciples, the means necessary for its salvific mission, which is a continuation of the mission of Christ. One aspect of that mission will be the forgiveness of sins.

These texts from Matthew and John root the Church's practice of the sacrament of reconciliation in the ministry of Jesus. They are not proof that Jesus initiated some formal ritual celebration of forgiveness, but rather texts that demonstrate that the Church's subsequent development of the ritual was consistent with Jesus' attitude to forgiveness. In the first two centuries of the Church there was no common, ritual practice of reconciliation.

One of the reasons for this lay in the fact that the early Christians believed that the Second Coming of Christ was imminent. Since baptism washed away sin, it was believed that there would be little chance to sin again before the Second Coming. In fact, the letter of James (written between AD 50–70) gives us an idea of the normal way of confession and intercessory prayer: 'So confess your sins to one another, and pray for one another' (James 5:16a). Christians were encouraged to confess to each other, praying together and correcting each other's faults. There was also a link with what we have seen earlier in our reflections on baptism in the early Church. Adults who were to become Christians underwent a lengthy period of preparation, sometimes two or three years, in which time they had to prove that they were ready to renounce sin and take on a new way of life. The celebration of reconciliation for these adult catechumens took the form of prayers and exorcism, freeing them from sin and praying they would not sin again.

However, things began to change with the persecution of Christians in the third century. Those who had renounced their faith in the face of persecution began to seek readmittance to the Christian community once the persecution was over. The Church was faced with the dilemma of welcoming back people who had sinned, were forgiven when they initially became Christians, but who had now sinned again in renouncing their faith. The Church had no set policy for such cases, and practices varied from those who demanded permanent excommunication for those who had renounced their faith to those more tolerant bishops who readmitted those who were genuinely sorry for what they had done. The era of persecution also saw the first stirrings of the debate about the distinction between serious sins and not-so serious sins. Nothing had been decreed, but there was a general consensus that idolatry, apostasy, adultery and fornication were serious (but there was no specific penance attached to them). The list has echoes in Paul's first letter to the people of Corinth, whom he said 'should not associate with a brother Christian who is leading an immoral life, or is a usurer, or idolatrous, or a slanderer, or a drunkard, or is dishonest; you should not even eat a meal with people like that' (1 Cor. 5:11). Origen, writing in the third century, used the term 'mortal sin' in reference to sins such as these which lost for the sinner the grace of the Holy Spirit received in baptism.

Canonical penance

Gradually, church practice suggested that forgiveness for mortal sins could only be obtained once after baptism and through a long and complicated process of penance. The first stage of this consisted of the sinner asking the bishop for forgiveness. This meant a confession in the presence of the bishop and some witnesses so that the bishop would know the sin committed and the state of the penitent (as late as the fifth century Pope Leo the Great reproved some Italian bishops for publicly reading from the pulpit the list of sins of those who had confessed to them). These sinners were now excluded from the Eucharist and were required to perform public acts of repentance. They became a class on their own, the *'paenitentes'*, forming the third class of Christians: the ordinary faithful, the catechumens, and the *'paenitentes'*. They were separated from the rest of the community, and in church had to sit in a corner set apart for them. This separation was a sign not of humiliation, but of the penitent's interior state of separation from God and the Church. The penitents were not completely separated from the community, however, for in some cases they would be assigned guardians to help them on their path to conversion once again, and the entire community prayed continually for them.

The second stage of the reconciliation process was the actual carrying out of the penance imposed by the bishop. Examples of this penance included lengthy prayers to be said on one's knees, fasting, alms-giving, wearing shirts made of goat's hair, or wearing chains (symbolising being tied to sin). While performing this penance, the sinner had to lead a life separate from the world, meaning no theatre-going, no banquets, no public baths, no military service, no undertaking of civil offices, no sexual relations, and no permission to get married.

This era became known as that of 'Canonical penance', because of the legal emphasis which governed the whole process. The rigorous canonical penance could last a few weeks or even many years (e.g. a seven-year penance for fornication, 15 years for idolatry) and was concluded in the final stage of the process, that of absolution and reconciliation. This usually took place at the end of Lent, on Holy Thursday. In front of the whole community the deacon would ask the bishop to give the grace of reconciliation to the penitents whose period of penance had ended. The bishop would exhort the penitents not to sin again, and lay his hands on them as a sign of their forgiveness by God. They were then readmitted to the Eucharist.

Canonical penance saw sin as something done against the community and it therefore warranted exclusion from that community. It reflected the belief that the bishops had the power to 'bind' and 'loose' and their declaration that a sinner was reconciled with the Church was the sign that he/she had also been forgiven by God. However, it also meant that sin was viewed very much in legal terms, with bishops acting as judges over the whole process. Sin was not so much breaking God's covenant of love but breaking a divine or church law. Repentance, therefore, was not so much conversion but completing the penalty imposed. The Church maintained that this forgiveness could only be obtained once, and so rather than encouraging penitents to be reconciled the process discouraged people from undergoing lengthy periods of penance in order to be forgiven. Many waited until they were dying before being reconciled, with a subsequent increase in 'death-bed confessions'. Reconciliation had become part of dying, not part of a Christian's life.

REFLECTION

- Automatic Confession Machines are, of course, invalid. But is there anything you think has become 'automatic' about the way we celebrate the sacrament of reconciliation today?
- The story of the Prodigal Son is well-known. What is your reaction to each of the characters: the younger son who asked for his share of the inheritance, the elder son who refused to join in the celebrations, and the father?
- Early church practice seems to suggest that sinners confessed to each other and turned to each other for correction and prayers. Do you think this would be possible today? What are the reasons for your answer?
- Canonical penance was full of symbolism, such as the class of *'paenitentes'*, and wearing clothes or chains symbolising sinfulness. This was due in part to the strong community

aspect of the sacrament, that sin was sin against the community. Do you see a community aspect in the sacrament of reconciliation today?

Tariffed penance

By the sixth century, penitential life in the Church was limited to the monastic way of life. Monks practised daily acts of penance, but more importantly they developed the idea of confessing sins to a 'soul friend', a kind of spiritual director. From such a guide they would receive penance and assurances of God's forgiveness. This practice spread in rural areas where the monks would visit and hear people's confession in private and suggest a penance. Until this had been accomplished, the penitent was to abstain from eucharistic communion, before returning, on the next visit from the monks, for absolution and reconciliation. Occasionally the latter would be given immediately, if someone had come a long way or it was likely that they would not see the monk again.

This practice maintained the stages of canonical penance (confession, penance, and absolution) and spread throughout Europe through the influence of Celtic monks. One particular characteristic of this Celtic practice was that the choice of penance was not left to the monk. 'Tariffs' were applied to each sin and these were contained in penitential books. For example, the penance for hitting somebody while talking to them was a 40-day fast (a year's fast for a cleric!); the penance for murder was compulsory exile; adultery incurred payment of damage to the injured party and total abstinence from sexual relations; theft called for a return of the stolen goods. Although less arduous than canonical penance, tariffed penance was still a burden, and the system was naturally open to negotiation and abuse. So, for example, a year's fasting could be altered to three day's complete abstinence from food and drink; or, even worse, a rich man required to fast for seven years could hire a small army to complete the fast in three days.

Another characteristic of the tariffed system of penance was that it was repeatable. It was possible to confess regularly, and furthermore the penance had no public obligations. By the end of the sixth century, the system had spread throughout most of Europe. It soon had immense success, despite initial opposition from local clergy. This way of celebrating the sacrament offered a way of being freed from the burden of sin without the heavy weight of canonical penance. Of course, penitential books still maintained a somewhat legalistic attitude to sin and reconciliation, and the monks were still cast in the role of judges who assigned the penance and decided when it had been completed. God was the judge who presided over this system of punishment for breaking divine and church laws.

Gradually, the practice of waiting to give absolution until the penance was completed was abolished. Many Christians took up the practice of confession without having any serious sins to confess, and bishops suggested periodical confession as a truly pious exercise. Eventually tariffs themselves disappeared, as it was felt that to have to accuse oneself of sin was bad enough. Penances were reduced to a few prayers, and the prayer of absolution became linked to the confession of sins, not to the completion of penance. It was also a prayer of absolution ('I absolve you . . .') replacing a prayer of forgiveness ('May God have mercy on you . . .'). The priest was not praying for God to forgive the sins, but was actually doing it in God's name, as his instrument. The order of the sacrament had now changed to confession, absolution and penance. The sacrament had also become private, with virtually no community dimension. Sin had become a private affair between the penitent and God, through the mediation of the priest. Private confession, on a regular basis, had become the norm, even though church law in some places still called for public penance.

The Fourth Lateran Council in 1215 responded to this situation: 'Every faithful of either sex who has reached the age of discretion should at least once a year faithfully confess all his sins in secret to his own priest.'[1] Annual confession was now an official sacrament of the Church. The decree of the Lateran Council put an end to the era of canonical and tariffed penance, and exhorted priests to maintain the 'seal of confession', with the punishment of removal from the priestly office and exclusion to a closed monastery for perpetual penance for those who broke it.

The decrees of the Fourth Lateran Council set the pattern for private sacramental confession for the next three hundred years. Debate continued among theologians over a number of matters, including the difference between 'venial' and 'mortal' sin. In the past, distinction was made between those sins that required public acts of penance and those that did not. In the Middle Ages, two types of sins were referred to: those that involved a complete rejection of God and would therefore incur eternal damnation, and those less serious sins which could be forgiven before God. 'Mortal' (from the Latin meaning 'deadly') sins were defined by St Thomas Aquinas as 'when our acts are so deranged that we turn away from our last end, namely God, to whom we should be united by charity'. 'Venial' sin did not involve such a fundamental rejection of God. Again, St Thomas Aquinas: 'Although a person who commits a venial sin does not actually refer his or her act to God, nevertheless he or she still keeps God as his or her habitual end. The person does not decisively set himself or herself on turning away from God, but from overfondness for a created good falls short of God. He or she is like a person who loiters, but without leaving the way.'

With sacramental practice now firmly fixed, attention focused on the individual elements of the sacrament, in an attempt to answer the question: what makes the sacrament of reconciliation? The first element was contrition, a genuine sorrow for sins committed. Aquinas believed that genuine contrition was needed for the sacrament to be effective, and genuine meant not a fear of divine retribution but a realisation that sin should have no place in a Christian way of life. The grace of the sacrament was the ability to have perfect contrition. The next element of the sacrament was the confession of sins, in private to a priest. This would gradually become a recitation or list of sins. The priest would then pronounce the words of absolution and prescribe a penance, to be completed afterwards by the penitent. In Aquinas' language, the actions of penitent and priest were the 'matter' of the sacrament, while the 'form' were the words of absolution, signifying divine forgiveness. This came from God, who, as we have seen in the gospel texts from

Matthew and John, entrusted his power to forgive sins to the apostles and then to his priests.

There were still a number of unanswered questions concerning the notion of penance, and they were often posed in the form of the dilemma of somebody dying before completing their penance. And if, as was now the case, forgiveness was given before the penance, what purpose did it serve? The scholastic answer was that absolution forgave the eternal punishment which sin incurred, but not the temporal punishment. Thus, penance on earth would still have to be done, and would have to be completed after death if it had not been completed on earth. This was the notion of 'purgatory', a place where sins could be purged. Aquinas also saw penance as a way of encouraging people to turn away from what he called the 'remnants of sin', the inclination to sin which remains despite forgiveness.

Other theologians of this time, however, saw the key to the sacrament as being absolution itself, with confession and contrition mere preconditions to receiving absolution. They were useful in helping the sacrament alter someone's way of life, but the only valid thing needed for the sacrament was absolution. Such a view coincided with the practice of penances that were now merely a few prayers, reducing any demand on the penitent. In this way, the sacrament of reconciliation had been invested with an almost magical quality with little or no effect on people's lives.

It was in such a climate that the practice of indulgences surfaced. Theologically, priests and bishops had the power to 'bind' and 'loose', to impose sanctions and release people from them. Starting in the eleventh century there had been a few cases where bishops granted release from certain amounts of penance yet to be completed to anyone who made a financial contribution to a particular church. In theory, such an indulgence was simply substituting for the penance still to be done, but it was interpreted as paying off all the penance to be done, both on earth and in purgatory. As the system became more popular, people would buy indulgences for their friends and relatives in purgatory, and in 1476 Pope Sixtus IV issued an indulgence specifically for this. But soon indulgences were being sold by bishops to earn certain positions within the Church, or to recruit warriors for the Crusades. In 1515 Pope Leo X announced an indulgence for the rebuilding of St Peter's Basilica in Rome. In Germany, the indulgence was proclaimed by Archbishop Albert of Mainz (also Archbishop of Magdeburg and administrator of the see of Halberstadt). To combine all these posts, he needed dispensations from Rome, and so he borrowed money to pay for these dispensations. The money the Archbishop then received from Leo X's indulgence went in part to St Peter's Basilica and in part to pay off his debts. The system of indulgences was wide open to corruption and the Protestant reformer Martin Luther spoke out against the whole practice: 'The Pope has wealth far beyond all other men – why does he not build St Peter's Church with his own money instead of the money of poor Christians?'

The Council of Trent

Luther wanted to reform the sacrament of penance, not eliminate it completely. He believed that undue emphasis on the sinner's penance made that seem more important than trust and faith in God's mercy. There had been a significant shift in the Church's understanding of the sacrament, with focus more on contrition, confession, absolution and penance than on the idea of reconciliation with God and the Church. But Luther was unsuccessful in his reforms and was excommunicated from the Catholic Church in 1520. (Many reformers saw little worth in the sacrament as envisaged by the Catholic Church and held that there was no scriptural basis for private confession, which slowly disappeared from most Protestant churches.)

The Council of Trent (1545–63) strongly reaffirmed the practice, ritual and discipline of confession as established by the Fourth Lateran Council more than three hundred years earlier. The bishops believed that private confession had been the practice of the Church from the outset and the Council of Trent provided a complete exposition of the structure and nature of the sacrament.

Quoting the passage from John's gospel (John 20:22ff.), the

bishops said that the sacrament was instituted by Christ and that for the full and perfect remission of sins three acts are required of the penitent: contrition, confession and satisfaction. Contrition involved not just acknowledgement of sinfulness but a desire to begin a new life; penitents, after careful self-examination, must confess all mortal sins 'specifically and in particular', while venial sins can be omitted without guilt and can be atoned for in other ways, since they do not exclude the penitent from the grace of God; and proportionate satisfaction, or penance, is there to detach penitents from sin, acting 'like a bridle to keep them in check, and make them more cautious and vigilant in the future.'[2]

The bishops were clear that all three elements were necessary for the sacrament. There could be no remission of sin without perfect contrition, which in fact brings about the immediate remission of sin. Since perfect contrition includes a fundamental choice for God, it therefore includes a desire for the sacrament. The absolution which follows renders the penitent just before God. It is an act which does not come from the priest, for he simply confers God's grace, the remission of sin. It is interesting that the statements on absolution are all couched in legal language, even declaring that absolution 'has the pattern of a judicial act in which the priest pronounces sentence as judge.'[3] To judge wisely, the priest needed all the evidence from the penitent, confirming the Council's view of the judgemental nature of the sacrament. It was an exercise of the power entrusted in the priest, and the sacrament of penance was seen in the context of justification, the process whereby a penitent becomes just and holy before God.

The Council of Trent had rooted the sacrament of penance firmly in the Church's legislation. The ideas of reconciliation and healing had gone, to be replaced by the strict statements requiring confession at least once a year and certainly after committing a mortal sin. And this was to remain the norm throughout the Catholic Church for the next four hundred years.

REFLECTION

- Tariffed penance was so-called because every sin earned a prearranged amount of penance. What penance would you give for: murder, theft, gluttony, impure thought, adultery? Would such penances be aimed at healing the penitent or punishing the sinner?
- How significant do you think it is that absolution originally came after penance was completed? What has been lost or gained by placing absolution before penance?
- The *Catechism of the Catholic Church* states: 'Mortal sin destroys charity in the heart of man by a grave violation of God's law; it turns man away from God, who is his ultimate end and his beatitude, by preferring an inferior good to him';[4] 'One commits venial sin when, in a less serious matter, one does not observe the standard prescribed by the moral law, or when one disobeys the moral law in a grave matter, but without full knowledge or without complete consent'.[5] What comments would you make on these statements?
- The Council of Trent set the norm for the sacrament of confession for centuries. What image of God do you think the emphasis on legislation suggests? Think of any Acts of Contrition that you know – what image of God do they project?

'Bless me, Father, for I have sinned'

For four hundred years, little changed as far as confession was concerned. Private confession was made even more private following the work of St Charles Borromeo (1538–84), who designed a confessor's chair surrounded by screens. This design lasted for some years before it was made compulsory, in 1614, for priests to hear confessions from behind a screen. This was partly to preserve anonymity but also to protect women from being solicited in the confessional. On the whole, confession remained a once-a-year experience, part of the preparation for the once-a-year receiving of communion. For such people, confession was an almost magic ritual required by church law.

Such a general picture needs to be tempered with the success of a number of saints who are renowned for the hours they spent hearing confessions. The most famous example must be St John Vianney (1786–1859), the Curé d'Ars, who regularly spent twelve hours a day in the confessional. For the sort of people who flocked to him and other similar priests and monks, confession was a deeply spiritual experience where they received counselling and a moving experience of the mercy of God.

More frequent confession came about after 1903, when Pope Pius X encouraged people to receive communion regularly. On the whole, people presumed that if they were receiving communion more than once a year they would have to go to confession more than once a year, in fact every time before going to communion. In 1910, Pope Pius X also decreed that children could receive communion from the age of reason, generally held to be seven; and since it was general practice to go to confession before communion, it was inevitable that children were encouraged to go to confession. With Pope Pius XI's 1943 exhortation to frequent devotional confession, the scene had been set for a picture recalled at the start of this reflection on the sacrament: row upon row of people waiting to go to confession on Saturday afternoon; watching to see the light go green as somebody comes out, and then nervously going in to begin 'Bless me, Father, for I have sinned'. Frequent confession may have resulted in a regular 'shopping list' of sins: 'I have sworn, told lies, and said God's name in vain, and I am sorry for all the sins I cannot now remember.' It was very much a private sacrament, in a darkened box, which only the priest could hear. After a few words of encouragement, he would give a penance which might entail a few prayers, and then he would recite the 'magic' words of absolution. The soul was white again.

Such generalisations are dangerous, and it would be wrong to suggest that confession was thus for everybody. For many, the sacrament remained a spiritual encounter with the merciful God who welcomed back the Prodigal. But it would be true to say that in the 1960s and 1970s numbers regularly confessing their sins began to decline. The reasons for this are many, complex, and inexhaustible, but there was clearly some unease about the legal, scholastic ideas which still provided the framework for confession. Society was changing fast, and within the Church there was a renewed interest in the Scriptures, which suggested that sin in the biblical sense had more to do with breaking a covenant relationship with God than breaking laws. It was more difficult to categorise sin according to mortal or venial and which law had been broken, as shown by the examples that eating meat on Friday and missing Mass on Sunday were mortal sins and as such merited eternal punishment.

The Second Vatican Council opened a window on the Church and let new light into many of its practices. The bishops heard how much the sacrament of penance/confession had changed down the centuries and responded to the pleas for its reform. Although the Council did not provide any detailed teaching on the sacrament, it pointed the way ahead in some enlightening statements: 'The rites and formulas of Penance are to be revised so that they more clearly express both the nature and effect of the sacrament';[6] 'Those who approach the sacrament of Penance obtain pardon through God's mercy for the offense committed against him, and are, at the same time, reconciled with the church which they have wounded by their sins and which by charity, by example and by prayer labors for their conversion';[7] 'By Baptism priests make men and women part of the people of God; by the sacrament of Penance they reconcile sinners with God and the church'.[8] With the community aspect returning to the fore, the bishops appointed a liturgical commission which resulted in the new *Rite of Penance*, published in 1973 to replace the Tridentine Rite of 1614.

Rite of Penance

The new *Rite of Penance* in fact offers three rites: the traditional private confession, a communal celebration, and a rite of reconciliation for several penitents with 'General Confession and Absolution'. The emphasis is very much on reconciliation, rather than absolution, with frequent use of Scripture texts to stimulate an examination of conscience.

One of the first changes to be noticed was the possibility of 'open' or 'face-to-face' confession. This immediately suggested that the emphasis was to be on pastoral counselling and spiritual guidance rather than judgement. Other changes in the individual rite suggested a Scripture passage be read by priest or penitent before the confession of sins, that the penance offered by the priest should correspond to the seriousness and nature of the sins, and for the 'Prayer of Sorrow' (what used to be termed the 'Act of Contrition') the *Rite of Penance* offers 14 alternatives.

The communal/individual form of celebration is offered in the context of a celebration of the Word of God. The Liturgy of the Word acts as a guide for reflection, with those present then encouraged to go and confess to the priests present. They receive individual penance and absolution and the service ends with a prayer of praise and thanksgiving to God.

The third form offered is a *Rite for Reconciliation of Several Penitents with General Confession and Absolution*. This rite, too, is in the context of a celebration of the Word. It is reserved for circumstances in which there are large numbers of penitents or insufficient time for individual confessions. The people are invited to confess their sins to God in their hearts, and then the priest presiding over the assembly prays for God's forgiveness and absolves those present. Various stipulations attached to this rite include the need for anyone with serious sin to go to individual confession as soon as possible, and certainly before another service of General Absolution.

The *Rite of Penance* was warmly welcomed in many parts of the world. Gone was the legal framework which had underpinned confession for so long. The emphasis was pastoral: 'By receiving repentant sinners and leading them to the light of the truth, the confessor fulfils a paternal function: he reveals the heart of the Father and reflects the image of Christ the Good Shepherd.'[9] And throughout, the Word of God, not a list of do's and don'ts, is the guide to many of the reflections offered in the new *Rite of Penance*.

Today, the *Rite of Penance* is still used in many of the Reconciliation Services that are popular in Lent and Advent. The *Rite of General Confession and Absolution* has effectively disappeared following further norms laid down in the 1983 *Code of Canon Law,* which stated that there must be a 'grave necessity' for such services to take place, and that such a service becomes invalid if the penitent does not make an individual confession of any serious sins in due time. In this case, the validity of the absolution depends on the penitent. Behind this decision lay the fear that general confession and absolution might replace individual confession as the norm.

But there is still much that is to be rediscovered in the *Rite of Penance*. Reconciliation begins with God, it is his initiative. Perhaps in the past the emphasis was on the penitent owning up to breaking certain laws. 'Jesus, however, not only exhorted people to repentance so that they would abandon their sins and turn wholeheartedly to the Lord, but welcoming sinners, he actually reconciled them with the Father.'[10] Reconciliation is about responding to God's call to 'turn back'.

In the past there was also great emphasis on sin and self-accusation. Many popular prayer books contained lists of sins for a detailed 'Examination of Conscience'. The *Rite of Penance* focuses on God's merciful love for us: '. . . the sinner who by the grace of a merciful God embraces the way of penance comes back to the Father who "first loved us" (1 John 4:19), to Christ who gave himself up for us, and to the Holy Spirit who has been poured out on us abundantly.'[11] God loved us first. Such a statement is a far-step removed from the idea that we could earn God's love by obeying all the rules. In fact, he loves us first, and it is only through that love that we can obtain forgiveness.

Nor is the sacrament to be seen in isolation, it is not something that can be ticked off as 'done' for that month. Reconciliation is part of the whole life of the Church, leading to a further celebration: 'The expression of all this is the sharing in the Lord's table, begun again or made more ardent; such a return of children from afar brings great rejoicing at the banquet of God's Church.'[12]

In a sense, the wheel has come full circle and we are back at the community aspect of reconciliation. The *Rite of Penance* is part of the Church's liturgy, the public worship of the Church not the private celebration of individuals:

> The whole Church, as a priestly people, acts in different ways in the work of reconciliation that has been entrusted to it by the Lord. Not only does the Church call sinners to repentance by preaching the word of God, but it also intercedes for them and helps penitents with maternal care and solicitude to acknowledge and confess their sins and to obtain the mercy of God, who alone can forgive sins. Further, the Church becomes itself the instrument of the conversion and absolution of the penitent through the ministry entrusted by Christ to the apostles and their successors.[13]

The ministry of reconciliation is that of the whole Church. The entire community is called upon to provide an environment that reconciles and forgives.

REFLECTION

- The changes in the sacrament down the centuries are reflected in the way the very name of the sacrament has changed: it has been penance, confession, and reconciliation. What do you think each name says?
- Anonymous confession and the modern 'Reconciliation rooms' – what are the advantages and disadvantages of each?
- What is your experience of Reconciliation Services according to the *Rite of Penance*? Have they helped in any way?
- Here are two alternative Prayers of Sorrow from the *Rite of Penance*. What does each say about God?

  O my God, I am sorry and beg pardon for all my sins, and detest them above all things, because they deserved your dreadful punishment, because they have crucified my loving Saviour Jesus Christ, and, most of all, because they offend your infinite goodness; and I firmly resolve, by the help of your grace, never to offend you again, and carefully to avoid the occasions of sin.

Lord God, in your goodness have mercy on me: do not look on my sins, but take away all my guilt. Create in me a clean heart and renew within me an upright spirit.

- Normal practice is that confession is celebrated before communion. With regards to children of seven or eight years old, how far do you think they can appreciate the richness of the sacrament of reconciliation?

Catholics and sin

'Modern Catechism Adds to Catalogue of Sins.' This was how one national newspaper greeted the publication of the *Catechism of the Catholic Church* in 1992 (French edition), stating that the Church had added 'tax evasion, drunken or dangerous driving and drug-trafficking to the modern catalogue of sins'. The notion that there are 'new' sins is, of course, mistaken, but our attitude to sin is central to how we look at the sacrament of reconciliation today. Many commentators would argue that the real reason so few people now celebrate the sacrament of reconciliation is because they have lost a sense of sin.

When the sacrament was popularly called 'confession', the emphasis was precisely that: owning up to breaking laws, possibly in order to avoid punishment (and it must be asked if this is what the sacrament still means to most seven and eight-year olds?). Such a view is limiting, because it does not take into account a relationship with God and with other people. Furthermore, it runs the risk of approaching the sacrament without even thinking about God and others, because the sacrament is viewed purely in terms of law.

But sin is really breaking a bond of love with God and with others, it is hurting others by our actions. To take a simple, yet common example: gossiping. It may seem trivial, but gossiping about someone else shows how we view others. It also shows how we view ourselves, since gossiping can often be done in order to be 'in' with the right group. It raises the question why do we need to do such things to make ourselves look better?

The basis for our attitude to sin is relationships: our relationship to ourselves, to others and to God. Sin is manipulation of others and of God for our own self-interest. But perhaps it is more helpful to say that we do not so much commit sins as fall into a condition of sinfulness. Sin is about who we are, not what we do. Our life-style and priorities in life reflect so much about us. Hence a great deal is made today about how we treat others, responding to Jesus' call to 'love your neighbour as yourself'. By doing nothing, we are falling into the sin of not loving others. It was once said that the easiest way for evil to triumph in this world is for good people to do nothing.

Sinfulness, then, grows out of an attitude in our lives, not out of an examination of certain laws. Approaching the sacrament of reconciliation, the fundamental question is not 'What have I done?' but 'What sort of person am I?'

It is called the sacrament of conversion
because it makes sacramentally present
Jesus' call to conversion,
the first step in returning to the Father
from whom one has strayed by sin.
It is called the sacrament of penance,
since it consecrates the Christian sinner's
personal and ecclesial steps of
conversion, penance and satisfaction
It is called the sacrament of confession,
since the disclosure or confession of sins
to a priest is an essential element
of this sacrament.
In a profound sense it is also a 'confession' –
acknowledgement and praise –
of the holiness of God
and of his mercy towards sinful man.
It is called the sacrament of forgiveness,
since by the priest's sacramental absolution
God grants the penitent 'pardon and peace'.

It is called the sacrament of reconciliation,
because it imparts to the sinner
the love of God who reconciles:
'Be reconciled to God'.
He who lives by God's merciful love
is ready to respond to the Lord's call:
'Go; first be reconciled to your brother'.
(*Catechism of the Catholic Church*)[14]

7 *Anointing of the Sick*

'What's in a name?' In *Romeo and Juliet* Shakespeare wrote something about a name and a rose, and the importance of the name can be seen as we reflect on the sacrament we today call the anointing of the sick. It used to be referred to as the last rites or extreme unction, with all that that conjures up about being at death's door. Last rites was a sign that medicine could do no more. It was very much a sacrament for those close to death and some old catechisms even gave the example that somone about to be executed could not receive extreme unction . . . you had to wait until they had been executed and were dying!

As we will see, the sacrament has gone from being a general anointing of the sick to the exclusive preserve of the dying and back again. It addresses that most fundamental of questions concerning the whole idea of suffering in the world. Much suffering and sickness immediately provokes the question 'Why?' The medical world attempts to provide medical answers and solutions that will make suffering more bearable. In a sense, the sacrament of the sick attempts to provide a spiritual support, a way of coping with suffering, as Christ's presence strengthens those afflicted with illness.

The healing ministry of Jesus

Jesus' ministry was certainly one of healing as the gospels present us with many vivid accounts of the healing miracles he performed: the paralytic let down through the roof, blind Bartimaeus, the deaf mute, and many more. Matthew's gospel tells how Jesus 'went round the whole of Galilee teaching in their synagogues, proclaiming the Good News of the kingdom and curing all kinds of diseases and sickness among the people. His fame spread throughout Syria, and those who were suffering from diseases and painful complaints of one kind or another, the possessed, epileptics, the paralysed, were all brought to him, and he cured them' (4:23–4). These healings are seen not only as proof of Jesus' divine mission but also as an essential part of his message: that the kingdom of God is present, his victory over sin and its consequences has already begun. (For many Jews there was a direct connection between sickness and illness, as seen by the disciples' question in John's gospel, 'Rabbi, who sinned, this man or his parents, for him to have been born blind?' (9:2).)

Jesus also entrusted the power to heal to his disciples: 'He called the Twelve together and gave them power and authority over all devils and to cure diseases, and he sent them out to proclaim the kingdom of God and to heal' (Luke 9:1–2). Indeed, his last words recorded in Mark's gospel state: 'These are the signs that will be associated with believers: in my name they will cast out devils; they will have the gift of tongues; they will pick up snakes in their hands and be unharmed should they drink deadly poison; they will lay their hands on the sick, who will recover' (16:17–18).

This healing ministry continued in the early Church, with Peter curing a cripple at the Beautiful Gate in Jerusalem (Acts 3:1–10) and a paralytic at Lydda (9:32–5), Philip curing several people in Samaria (8:7), and Paul curing the sick who were brought to him in Malta (28:7–10).

The practice in Jerusalem is reflected in the letter of James, the leader of the Christian community there: 'If one of you is ill, he should send for the elders of the church, and they must anoint him with oil in the name of the Lord and pray over him. The prayer of faith will save the sick man and the Lord will raise him up again; and if he has committed any sins, he will be forgiven' (5:14–15).

This passage has clear similarities with anointing as it is today, and many features are worthy of comment. There is no suggestion that the ill person is close to death, indeed if the sick person is to call the elders that would suggest quite the opposite. The 'elders', those in charge of the community, are the ones who anoint, and this includes praying over the sick person, almost in a literal sense (implying an imposition of hands). The fact that this is all done 'in the name of the Lord', at the command of Christ, shows that this is very much a religious act, not a medicinal one. The salvation brought about by this act included not only the possibility of physical healing but also salvation for the soul. The author of the letter seems to be suggesting any salvation which is necessary for the sick person. The prayer and anointing bring true salvation, enabling the Christian to bear suffering at such a time. As the final verse of the passage states, the anointing also remits any sin.

In the letter of James, then, we have a ritual act of prayer and anointing. This passage was to be the key text for claiming that the sacrament of anointing was instituted by Christ. For the action here is consistent with the whole of Jesus' public ministry, as he brought comfort to the sick and healed many who were ill. Christ also entrusted this task to his disciples, and so in the passage from the letter of James the Church is simply fulfilling the mission entrusted to it by Christ.

For the next few centuries there is little evidence of a set pattern for healing and anointing in the Church. Many people would bring to church oil to be blessed by the bishop, who prayed that 'it may give strength to all who taste it and strength to all who use it'. If anyone was then ill at home, the people had the oil ready for anointing. The efficacy of the oil and the healing was attributed either to the blessing of the oil itself or to the holiness of the one who applied it. Thomas Aquinas tells the story of St Genevieve of Paris, who in the fourth century used to visit the sick and anoint them with oil blessed by the bishop, and in this way she healed many people.

The first clear statement about anointing and healing is contained in a letter from Pope Innocent I to the Bishop of Gubbio, in Italy. This letter, dating from 416, is a summary of contemporary ideas. Quoting the letter of James, the Pope declares: 'This must undoubtedly be accepted and understood as referring to the oil of Chrism, prepared by the bishop, which can be used for anointing not only by priests but also by all Christians whenever they themselves or their people are in need of it.'[1]

Pope Innocent I also pointed out that those still completing penances could not be anointed, 'for it is of the nature of a sacrament', and since they could not receive the other sacraments they could not be anointed either. The two anointings, by priests or lay people, continued for the next few centuries. Pope Innocent had referred to it as a sacrament, for it symbolised the healing power of the Holy Spirit.

Many of the lives of the saints and holy people contain stories of miraculous cures brought about by anointing with blessed oil. Such stories, be they true or not, encouraged people to ask for anointing to cure any type of illness. Interestingly enough, nobody asked to be anointed if they were dying, instead they asked for Eucharist and reconciliation. This was the era of death-bed confessions, and the ritual included an anointing reserved to the priest alone. Some interpreted the passage from the letter of James to refer to this.

In the ninth century, priests were encouraged to carry the oil with them at all times, in case it was needed, and many bishops forbade lay people from anointing. The sacrament became clericalised once it became clear that it was a sacrament about forgiveness rather than healing. Only priests could forgive and forgiveness could only be given once. More and more, anointing became associated with death, even though the prayers still spoke of healing. There were very practical reasons for this. People who confessed their sins did not want to incur burdensome penances, and so delayed confession as long as possible. The elaborate rituals devised for the blessing and administration of oil required the presence of at least three priests, with various roles of sprinkling with holy water, reciting psalms, and anointing with ashes and oil. The tradition was that each priest took a stipend, and many people could not afford this. Furthermore, Pope Innocent I had said that penitents should not be anointed, and so church practice gradually moved towards confession, anointing and then viaticum (from the Latin 'provision for a journey'), the last communion. These were to become the 'last rites'.

Anointing had now become a preparation for death. Healing was no longer expected and the prayers of healing were dropped from the ritual. The order in the ritual also changed, with anointing coming after confession and communion. It was the last anointing people would receive, the 'extreme unction'. This name for the sacrament would remain in place for a long time.

REFLECTION

- Have you any experience of being anointed or attending a 'Service of Anointing'? What effect do you think it had?
- Many of the healing miracles of Jesus are memorable, since they entail physical healing. Do you think that was the only type of healing Jesus accomplished? What other types of healing do you think he brought?

What happened in extreme unction?

By the twelfth century, what began as a sacrament of healing had become a consecration for death. It was administered when death was imminent, with the prayer 'Through this holy anointing and his tender mercy, may the Lord forgive whatever sins you may have committed by sight, by hearing . . .', and so on as various parts of the body were anointed. The sacrament could only be received once and the principal condition for receiving it was danger of death.

But some theologians immediately pointed to the fact that the prayer of anointing asked for forgiveness when there was already a different sacrament for that, and, furthermore, anointing was the last element of a ritual that also included confession anyway. So what happened in extreme unction?

Thomas Aquinas believed that extreme unction destroyed the 'remnants of sin', the inclination to sin which would prevent someone from entering the perfection of heaven. It was the last time Christians would be offered the grace to overcome sin in preparation for entry into eternal life and the vision of God. Of course, the sick person had to co-operate with God's grace by inwardly rejecting sin and turning to God. (Aquinas therefore believed that children and those unable to understand the words of the rite could not be anointed, since they would be unable to co-operate with God's grace). In effect, extreme unction removed all obstacles barring the way to heaven. Despite this, many people still did not receive the sacrament. It was costly, with the priest expecting a stipend, and since the sacrament had to be administered as close to death as possible people might die before a priest arrived.

The sacramentality of all this was denied by the Protestant reformers, who stated that Christ did not institute anointing. Luther pointed out that the letter of James referred to an anointing for healing, whereas present practice was anointing for death. Calvin spoke of the whole idea as 'hypocritical play acting' by priests.

The Catholic Church's response at the Council of Trent was a clear statement, the *Doctrine on the Sacrament of Extreme Unction* (1551). The bishops stated that the sacrament was instituted by Christ and its effect was to take away sin and the remains of sin:

> It comforts and strengthens the soul of the sick person by awakening in him great confidence in the divine mercy; supported by this, the sick bears more lightly the inconveniences and trials of his illness and resists more easily the temptations of the devil who lies in wait . . .; at times it also restores bodily health when it is expedient for the salvation of the soul.[2]

The sacrament is to be administered 'to the sick, especially to those who are so dangerously ill that they seem to be near death'.[3]

Extreme unction brought purification, conferring grace, forgiving sins, and comforting the sick. Although the Council of Trent acknowledged that the sacrament was available for all the sick, it continued to be seen as exclusively for the dying. A standard, simplified rite was established in 1614 and little else changed for more than three hundred years. In that time certain questions were resolved, notably that of whether the dead could be anointed. Canon lawyers provided the answer that since it was difficult to determine the exact moment of death, those who were 'apparently' dead should be conditionally anointed in case the soul was still within the body.

Extreme unction was meant to be a sacrament confirming the Church's view that death was not the end but preparation for a new life. In anointing, a person was being entrusted to a merciful God, and the sacrament was an attempt to show that this transition is filled with hope. But in practice, this was not the case. Extreme unction, the last rites, was linked more with imminent death rather than the hope of new life. Calling out a priest to administer the sacrament was the ultimate sign that there was to be no recovery. There was some irony in the fact that at the very time when the Church's ministry was needed most of all, fear of death may have prevented people from celebrating the presence of Jesus in the sacrament of anointing.

In the early part of this century such a view began to be challenged. Once again, a renewal in biblical scholarship showed how much more positive the New Testament experience of and reflection on death was, compared to the sombre, mournful funerals celebrated in churches. There were calls for this sacrament not to be restricted to the dying.

At the Second Vatican Council, the bishops responded to these calls:

> Extreme Unction, which may also and more fittingly be called 'Anointing of the Sick', is not a sacrament intended only for those who are at the point of death. Hence, it is certain that as soon as any of the faithful begins to be in danger of death from sickness or old age, this is already a suitable time for them to receive this sacrament.[4]

The bishops also restored the order in the rite to confession, anointing, and viaticum, and called for a new rite to be prepared.

Pastoral Care of the Sick – Rites of Anointing and Viaticum was approved by Pope Paul VI in 1972. A dramatic change was noted immediately in the very title, for the whole ministry was now being placed in the context of pastoral care, a much broader spectrum than administering to the dying. Nor is the ministry just anointing, but it includes everything that comes under a potential heading of 'care for the sick'. The new rite offers a variety of celebrations using a number of texts. Anointing can be done at home, in a hospital, in a communal celebration, for the dying, for those with less serious illnesses, and as often as people might benefit from it. Underlying the entire rite are notions of healing and strengthening: 'Through this holy anointing may the Lord in his love and mercy help you with the grace of the Holy Spirit. May the Lord who frees you from sin save you and raise you up.'

Sickness can often bring with it a sense of isolation and loneliness. The new rite attempts to return to the effect Jesus had on those he healed. Those he met were astounded not only by the fact that he healed but also that he touched people. Jesus still touches and comes to those who are ill or dying, removing the sense of loneliness and isolation.

What is perhaps still unclear, however, is the real theology of illness. In other words, is illness a preparation for heaven, suffering in this life in order to be rewarded in the next, or is it just a normal part of human life? Does illness make us more like Jesus, uniting us to his suffering? Some would argue that anointing of the dying is the sacrament which conforms us to Christ, who has already gone through death and is with the Father. Anointing of the sick gives a Christian meaning to illness.

The *Catechism of the Catholic Church* acknowledges the special role those who are ill can have in the life of the Church: 'By the sacred anointing of the sick and the prayer of the priests the whole Church commends those who are ill to the suffering and glorified Lord, that he may raise them up and save them. And indeed she exhorts them to contribute to the good of the People of God by freely uniting themselves to the Passion and death of Christ'[5]; 'By his Passion and death on the cross Christ has given a new meaning to suffering: it can henceforth configure us to him and unite us with his redemptive Passion'[6]; 'Suffering, a consequence of original sin, acquires a new meaning; it becomes a participation in the saving work of Jesus'[7]; 'By celebrating this sacrament the Church, in the communion of saints, intercedes for the benefit of the sick person, and he, for his part, through the grace of this sacrament, contributes to the sanctification of the Church and to the good of all men for whom the Church suffers and offers herself through Christ to God the Father'.[8]

As regards the ministry to those who are ill, the *Pastoral Care of the Sick* makes it clear that ministering to them is the responsibility of the whole community:

> It is . . . especially fitting that all baptised Christians share in this ministry of mutual charity within the Body of Christ by doing all that they can to help the sick return to health, by showing love for the sick, and by celebrating the sacraments with them. Like the other sacraments, these too have a community aspect, which should be brought out as much as possible when they are celebrated.[9]

It must be remembered that all sacraments are the action of God. In the sacrament of anointing, therefore, we are celebrating God's love for us. His love does not cease because of illness, rather the sacrament is an example of his unending compassion. God's action emphasises life, not death, and with his grace may come the gift of health. If that is not the case God's action is still life-giving, only the focus is now on the life to come.

It is fitting, then, that the sacramental presence of Jesus be celebrated close to death with viaticum, the sacrament of the dying:

> The celebration of the Eucharist as viaticum, food for the passage through death to eternal life, is the sacrament proper to the dying Christian. It is the completion and crown of the Christian life on this earth, signifying that the Christian follows the Lord to eternal glory and the banquet of the heavenly kingdom. The sacrament of the anointing of the sick should be celebrated at the beginning of a serious illness. Viaticum, celebrated when death is close, will then be better understood as the last sacrament of Christian life.[10]

REFLECTION

- What image does the phrase 'Extreme Unction' conjure up? In the Middle Ages do you think the sacrament was about healing or forgiveness?
- *Pastoral Care of the Sick* makes it clear that such a ministry

is the responsibility of the whole community. What roles do you think people might play? How might a parish team of 'Visitors to the Sick and the Dying' operate?

- The theology of sickness is unclear. Do you think it is sufficient to ask people to 'offer it up to God' as their cross to bear, on the grounds that suffering in this life could lead to rewards in the next? What message would you give to someone who is ill or dying? If you were in such a position what would you like to hear?
- What effect can anointing have not only on the one anointed but also on those witnessing the sacrament? Is it a means of strengthening and healing for all?

Dear friends,
there is no force or power
that can block God's love for you.
Sickness and suffering seem to contradict
all that is worthy, all that is desired by man.
And yet no disease, no injury, no infirmity
can ever deprive you of your dignity as
children of God, as brothers and sisters of Jesus Christ.
. . . The anointing is therefore a source of strength
for both the soul and the body.
The prayer of the Church asks that sin and the
remnants of sin be taken away.
It also implores a restoration of health,
but always in order that bodily healing
may bring greater union with God
through the increase of grace.

Today I make an urgent plea to this nation.
Do not neglect your sick and elderly.
Do not turn away from the handicapped and the dying.
Do not push them to the margins of society.
For if you do, you will fail to understand that they
represent an important truth.
The sick, the elderly, the handicapped and the dying
teach us that weakness is a creative part of human living,

and that suffering can be embraced with no loss of dignity.
Without the presence of these people in your midst
you might be tempted to think of health, strength and power
as the only important values to be pursued in life.
But the wisdom of Christ and the power of Christ are
to be seen in the weakness of those who share his sufferings.

(John Paul II)[11]

8 Holy Orders

'Nothing is so irritating as being lectured by ecclesiastics on matters outside their competence', said a national newspaper article responding to *The Common Good*, a document on the Catholic Church's social teaching published by the Catholic Bishops of England and Wales. 'Who needs these meddlesome priests?', said another. 'In theory, they [bishops] are chosen by the Pope. In reality, they become bishops after secret consultations involving tiny numbers of ecclesiastical busybodies and bureaucrats. Ordinary Catholics are not consulted, and that is typical of how Catholic bishops behave in their own affairs.' For some time the debate about the role of priests and bishops continued to fill our newspapers. 'The only economy the bishops should be concerned with is the economy of salvation', was another blunt comment.

Not all the comments were negative, however. Many people praised the bishops for their courageous step in expressing the Church's teaching on many of the key social issues of the day, saying it was right that reflection on society should be done in the light of gospel values. Christianity cannot keep silent on this.

Underlying this whole debate was a question about the role of those who are ordained. Should theirs be a purely spiritual role, concerned with 'churchy' things only? Or are they in a position to make the sort of comments that caused such national debate among people of all persuasions? It was once said that 'Sermons remain one of the last forms of public discourse where it is culturally forbidden to talk back'. One document from the bishops had thousands of people answering back, and I'm sure many had their own view on the fundamental question: What is the role of a priest?

Ministries – no priests?

The history of religions shows that nearly all religions have had a priest or equivalent figure, a holy person. Such a figure acted as a mediator between the deity and humanity, between the divine and the human. This is a two-way process, with the priest communicating with the people on behalf of the deity and vice-versa.

The Bible presents us with many such figures, performing a variety of functions. One such was Zechariah:

> In the days of King Herod of Judaea there lived a priest called Zechariah who belonged to the Abijah section of the priesthood . . . Now it was the turn of Zechariah's section to serve, and he was exercising his priestly office before God when it fell to him by lot, as the ritual custom was, to enter the Lord's sanctuary and burn incense there. And at the hour of incense the whole congregation was outside, praying. (Luke 1:5a, 8–10)

In Judaism, priesthood was hereditary, and Zechariah belonged to the section of priests descended from Abijah, one of the grandsons of the first high priest, Aaron.

In his life and ministry Jesus was certainly a mediator between God and humanity. From the outset, Jesus spoke of God's love and wishes for his people. Jesus brought God to the people, he was the Word made flesh: 'The time has come and the kingdom of God is close at hand. Repent, and believe the Good News' (Mark 1:15); 'Now the will of him who sent me is that I should lose nothing of all that he has given to me, and that I should raise it up on the last day. Yes, it is my Father's will that whoever sees the Son and believes in him shall have eternal life, and that I shall raise him up on the last day' (John 6:39–40); 'Anyone who wants to become great among you must be your servant, and anyone who wants to be first among you must be slave to all. For the Son of Man himself did not come to be served but to serve, and to give his life as a ransom for many' (Mark 10:42–5).

Jesus taught with authority, and he gave an example of leadership which involved service rather than power. He gathered around himself a band of followers, with a special calling addressed to the Twelve, who were with him during his life and witnessed his message and ministry. Following his death and resurrection, they continued the work of Jesus as he had asked them to: 'Go, therefore, make disciples of all the nations; baptise them in the name of the Father, and of the Son and of the Holy Spirit, and teach them to observe all the commands I gave you. And know that I am with you always; yes, to the end of time' (Matt. 28:19–20).

In the early Christian community in Jerusalem, the Twelve were central. In the Acts of the Apostles, the community bring their offerings and present them to the apostles for distribution among the needy (4:33–7); Saul is introduced to the apostles after his conversion (9:26–8); and the so-called Council of Jerusalem was presided over by the 'apostles and elders' (15:6).

The apostles clearly had authority in the early Church. But it is significant that their role is largely that of preaching:

> About this time, when the number of disciples was increasing, the Hellenists made a complaint against the Hebrews: in the daily distribution their widows were being overlooked. So the Twelve called a full meeting of the disciples and addressed them, 'It would not be right for us to neglect the word of God so as to give out food; you, brothers, must select from among yourselves seven men of good reputation, filled with the Spirit and with wisdom; we will hand over this duty to them, and continue to devote ourselves to prayer and to the service of the word'. (6:1–4)

Seven were chosen and presented to the Twelve, 'who prayed and laid their hands on them' (6:6). The chief work of the Twelve was prayer in the community and the ministry of the word, preaching the message of Christ.

Of course many others were working in the early Christian communities, and fortunately the nature of the work is easily described by the names given to the different workers. Some were *apostoloi*, the Greek word meaning 'ambassador', a term not referred exclusively to the Twelve but applied to those who spread the message of Christ; others were *episkopoi* or *presbyteroi*, elders or supervisors of the communities entrusted to them. And the work carried out by many was *diakonia*, a word meaning 'service'.

The terms *episkopoi* and *presbyteroi* are the roots of our words for 'bishop' and 'priest', but the work of these elders in the Christian community does not exactly reflect the role of bishops and priests as we understand those terms today. After an initial visit from an apostle, the care of communities was often entrusted to an elder or group of elders: 'In each of these churches they appointed elders, and with prayer and fasting they commended them to the Lord in whom they had come to believe' (Acts 14:23). The first letter to Timothy, written towards the end of the first century, outlines the necessary qualities of an elder:

> He must not have been married more than once, and he must be temperate, discreet and courteous, hospitable and a good teacher; not a heavy drinker, nor hot-tempered, but kind and peaceable. He must not be a lover of money. He must be a man who manages his own family well and brings his children up to obey him and be well-behaved; how can any man who does not understand how to manage his own family have responsibility for the church of God? He should not be a new convert, in case pride might turn his head and then he might be condemned as the devil was condemned. It is also necessary that people outside the Church should speak well of him, so that he never gets a bad reputation and falls into the devil's trap. (1 Tim. 3:2b–7)

Quite some list of qualifications!

A similar set of characteristics is applied in the same letter to those who serve the church as deacons: 'They must be conscientious believers in the mystery of the faith. They are to be examined first, and only admitted to serve as deacons if there is nothing against them. In the same way, the women must be respectable, not gossips but sober and quite reliable' (1 Tim. 3:9–11).

The picture of early church life that we find in the New Testament is one where a number of ministries are being carried out. Elders and deacons were appointed to their roles within the community, and numerous ministries flourished under their guidance. Widows performed a ministry of hospitality and good works (1 Tim. 5:9–16), we read of Priscilla and Aquila giving 'further instruction about the Way' (Acts 18:26), and people were encouraged to use their gifts within the community, gifts of prophecy, administration, teaching, preaching, alms-giving, and doing works of mercy (Rom. 12:3–8). What we do not come across in these ministries is any priestly ministry in the understanding of the word in Catholic circles today. There are perhaps two chief reasons for this: the early Christians continued to worship at the temple where the recognised Jewish priesthood was at work and priesthood was linked with the idea of sacrifices to God, which was not part of early Christian worship.

It is in this context that we must look at the Letter to the Hebrews, written shortly before the destruction of the Jerusalem Temple in AD 70. The author presents a clear vision of the priesthood and sacrifice of Christ which replaces the priesthood and sacrifices of Judaism. The basic standpoint is simple: unlike the continual sacrifices of Temple worship, Jesus' sacrifice on the cross has been made once and for all, and Jesus is both the perfect victim and the perfect priest offering the sacrifice. This is a new notion of priesthood, not descended from the line of Aaron, but from the line of Melchizedek, priest of the Most High God (Gen. 14:18):

> All the priests stand at their duties every day, offering over and over again the same sacrifices which are quite incapable of taking sins away. He, on the other hand, has offered one single sacrifice for sins, and then taken his place for ever, at the right hand of God, where he is now waiting until his enemies are made into a footstool for him. By virtue of that one single offering, he has achieved the eternal perfection of all whom he is sanctifying. (Heb. 10:11–14)

Jesus is the 'compassionate and trustworthy high priest of God's religion, able to atone for human sins' (2:17); he is the ideal high priest, 'holy, innocent and uncontaminated, beyond the influence of sinners, and raised up above the heavens; one who would not need to offer sacrifices every day, as the other high priests do for their own sins and then for those of the people, because he has done this once and for all by offering himself' (7:26–8).

This new ideal of high priest is also founded on a new covenant, mediated by Christ, between God and his people:

> But what you have come to is Mount Zion and the city of the living God, the heavenly Jerusalem where the millions of angels have gathered for the festival, with the whole Church in which everyone is a 'first-born-son' and a citizen of heaven. You have come to God himself, the supreme Judge, and been placed with the spirits of the saints who have been made perfect; and to Jesus, the mediator who brings a new covenant and a blood for purification which pleads more insistently than Abel's. (12:22–4)

The ancestral priesthood of Judaism had been replaced; here is an eternal priesthood, exercised through the offering of a unique and perfect sacrifice. Henceforth all priesthood would be seen to have its origins in the priesthood of Christ. For the early Church, Christ was *the* high priest of the new religion, and he had called together 'a chosen race, a royal priesthood, a consecrated nation, a people set apart to sing the praises of God who called you out of darkness into his wonderful light' (1 Pet. 2:9).

REFLECTION

- What is your image of priesthood? Do you think of priests in terms of what they are or what they do? Does one come before the other?
- In the life and ministry of Jesus, what qualities would you describe as 'priestly', in so far as we use the term today?
- What do you think is the connection between leadership, authority and service? How can these three qualities be seen in one person?
- In the early Church the emphasis was clearly on ministry,

responding to needs and using gifts. How useful is this concept of ministry arising from needs and gifts? What parallels can you see today in your parish or congregation?

- What are your thoughts on the new priesthood, the new covenant implied by the letter to the Hebrews? How is Jesus *the* high priest?

Bishops, deacons and priests

Gradually, a hierarchical structure emerged in the Church headed by bishops, deacons and priests. The elders were in charge of the communities, and as the liturgy developed the role of presiding at the Eucharist was reserved exclusively to them. In some communities the presiding elder was called an *episkopos*, 'bishop'. Other elders were referred to as *presbyteroi*, while others with a specific liturgical role were called *diakonoi*.

The bishop had overall responsibility for the local community. His authority was such that permission was needed from the bishop for anything relating to the Church and his approval was seen as a sign of God's approval. At the beginning of the second century, writers such as Ignatius of Antioch saw the bishop's role as essential in preserving doctrinal unity. It was important to hand on what the apostles had preached, and with this in mind the bishops began to see themselves as 'successors of the apostles'. Not to be at one with the bishop was interpreted as being outside the Church, since the bishops were seen as the only true teachers of the faith. The ministry of the bishop was varied: he presided at the Eucharist, he instructed catechumens, defended the Church and kept it free from heresy, and administered the affairs of the community.

The first assistants for bishops were deacons. Their role was both liturgical (reading and distributing communion) and administrative (collecting and distributing offerings to the needy and looking after church finances). Deacons served the bishop as his personal assistants and eventually performed some of the liturgical functions he was unable to do (e.g. anointings at baptism). They were the most powerful group in the community after the bishop himself. For the other elders in the community, the presbyters, there was little left to do. Occasionally they would preside at prayer services and act as a sort of parish council. When the bishop presided at the Eucharist, the elders would sit next to him and place their hands over the bread and wine at the same time as the bishop. But unlike bishops and deacons, presbyters did not have a full-time ministry. They had to have a job to support their family, while the faithful supported the bishop and his family.

By the third century formal ordination rituals were in place for the ministries of bishops, deacons, and presbyters. This consisted of laying on of hands and a prayer. For bishops, this was performed by the presbyters and other bishops; for presbyters, this was done by the bishop and other presbyters; and for deacons it was done simply by the bishop, since the deacon was his personal assistant and did not have the same rank as presbyter.

Although elders and bishops were still, for the most part, elected by the community, the ordination rite set apart bishops, deacons and priests from the community. As their functions became more and more specialised they were seen as a separate order, and bishops and elders were referred to as 'priests'. By the end of the third century the ministries of bishop and presbyter (who fulfilled the liturgical role of the bishop in his absence) had become priestly ministries performed by sacred persons. Beneath the priestly ministries other ministries continued to flourish and were much needed as communities grew larger. 'Subdeacons' assisted deacons, and other ministries were performed by exorcists, lectors, porters, acolytes, and teachers.

In 313, the Edict of Milan put an end to the persecution of Christianity and by the end of the century Christianity had become the official religion of the Roman Empire. This was to have a dramatic effect on ministry in the Church. Communities increased and the bishop was no longer able to fulfil all his liturgical duties to satisfy the different communities. Although deacons and teachers could prepare catechumens there was still the problem of the Eucharist, which the bishop was unable to celebrate every week in all the communities. Presbyters were therefore appointed to preside at the Eucharist and to baptise. The ministry of the elders was now a priestly ministry. They acted independently of the bishop, but under his authority and with his permission. Presbyters did not take all the bishop's roles, however, and it was significant that the completion of Christian initiation, the final anointing with oil, was reserved to the bishop – the beginning of the separate sacrament of confirmation.

The term 'priest' gradually became the common term for bishops and presbyters, due in great part to their liturgical role. Occasionally, bishops would be referred to as 'high priests', but the difference between the two was seen in terms of authority. The bishop exercised greater authority in the Church and a certain amount of his work was taken up with administration. The priest was seen as the leader of a local community. One of the consequences of the emphasis on the liturgical role of priests and bishops was the disappearance of the deacon as a separate minister. They had acted as assistants to the bishops, but the need now was for ministers who presided at the Eucharist, and such a function was fulfilled by priests. In some areas bishops ordained deacons, and the diaconate came to be seen as a step on the road to priesthood. In time, even the ministries of subdeacon, porter, lector, exorcist, and acolyte were viewed as stages on the road to ordination as a priest. The order of clergy had become a graded series of orders, with ministry reserved only to those within that order. Since the clergy also received many of the privileges of those holding high office in the state (such as exemption from paying tax and from military service) the sharp division between clergy and laity was clear for all to see. The implication was that those in orders were better than others, and the authority they exercised came with the position.

Needless to say, these exalted positions brought not only privileges but also responsibilities. Clergy were *expected* to be better, holier than the laity. Bishops, especially, were expected to be good leaders in the Church and in the State, where many of them continued to exercise the role of magistrates. In this role they had to dress as judges, with a special gown. Thus distinctive clothing was to become a further sign of the separation between clergy and laity.

Up to now we have seen that the rise of the priestly ministry and its distinctive nature was largely a response to changing practical situations. It was not until the start of the fifth century that the nature of priesthood was reflected in the theological writings of great saints such as John Chrysostom (*c.* 347–407) and Augustine (354–430). They saw priests as God's instruments, working through them despite any failings they might have. God spoke through his priests and to reject them was to reject God. Ordination set them apart and transformed them with a special dignity. Augustine spoke of a spiritual 'character' of Christ the priest imprinted on the ordained, just like baptism imprinted a character. Ordination, like baptism, could not be repeated. The character was a sign of who the priest was, set aside so that God could work through him, and this reinforced the notion of *ex opere operato*, that a sacrament did not depend on the worthiness of the priest, since it was God at work through the priest. Furthermore, there was only one notion of priesthood, equally possessed by bishops and priests. The difference between bishops and priests was one of authority and jurisdiction, not one of priesthood. Theological reflection on ordination itself led to the conclusion that ordination through the laying on of hands was the work of the Holy Spirit, effecting a transformation in the ordained. Ordained bishops received the spiritual power to be teachers and leaders in the Church, and in turn they transmitted to priests the power to celebrate the Eucharist, to serve in God's Church, and to guide the local communities.

Priesthood was seen almost exclusively in liturgical terms. The effect on the liturgy was that it became the personal domain of the priest, an event which people watched rather than participated in. As the communities grew in number and therefore the need for more Masses increased, so priests were ordained simply to say Mass: 'Massing-priests'. But this liturgical role raised the whole question of worthiness and holiness, with the latter commonly associated with sexual purity. The elders of the early Christian communities were often chosen because they were able to manage their families well (1 Tim. 3:2b–7) and yet slowly the notion of abstinence from sexual relationships began to be associated with the ordained ministry. In the Temple priesthood of Judaism, priests had to abstain from sexual relations during their time of service. In the fourth century some church writers suggested the same should be applied to priests in the Church, or even extended to the idea of lifelong abstention, since priests were such for life. At this time most clergy were married, and it was increasingly held that on ordination they should henceforth refrain from sexual intercourse. However, the only way to impose such rules was to ordain only those who were not married.

REFLECTION

- The hierarchy of bishops, deacons and priests arose as communities grew. For the most part, these ministers were still elected by the community, chosen from among them. What advantages does such a choice have? Does the community have a similar role today?
- The term 'priest' came from the term 'presbyter', or elder. The ministry of elder began as someone on a type of parish council, an advisory role. Priestly ministry became associated with presiding at the Eucharist. Are there two types of ministry here, now vested in one person? How separate should they be?
- Ordination was a sign that those ordained were of a different rank, of the 'order of priests'. The word 'order' here simply describes a group subject to certain religious rules. How useful is the division between clergy and laity? In what ways is it most apparent today?
- Celibacy slowly began to replace continence as an ideal. What do you think is the positive reason for this, and how would you comment on celibacy in the light of the recommendations in the first letter of Timothy that a bishop must be 'a man who manages his family well and brings his children up to obey him and be well-behaved' (2:4)?

Power, authority and celibacy

In the Middle Ages, the Christian faith spread throughout Europe. Missionary monks were sent out from Rome, perhaps the most famous group being the monks sent by Pope

Gregory the Great (*c.* 540–604) to convert the Anglo-Saxons. Augustine of Canterbury set out from Rome in 596 accompanied by 29 other monks to evangelise the Anglo-Saxons. Similar initiatives took place throughout Europe, and the bishops began to see themselves as spiritual leaders of the whole of society. They were Christ's representatives on earth. From the fifth century the bishop of Rome was viewed with special importance, since many churches in Europe had been founded by missionaries sent from Rome. Peter had been the first bishop of Rome, and now his successor was seen as the most important bishop.

As the feudal system spread throughout Europe, many churches became wealthy landowners. The feudal system was basically one of allegiance to those above you, with peasants at the bottom and landowners and rulers at the top. Bishops fitted into this picture with their vast dioceses which brought in much-needed revenue, as they looked after the material and spiritual needs of the clergy and faithful. Although spiritual authority and temporal power were separate areas, they in fact often became united, since some bishops were related to the temporal lords and were even appointed by them. In order to retain its property, the Church preferred celibate bishops.

The chief role of the bishop had become administrative. In the later Middle Ages many of the bishops were very wealthy, and the office of bishop was often a reward of high birth or administrative skill. A bishop exercised power on his lands, collecting taxes, looking after church and farm buildings, and carrying out other such tasks. Occasionally a bishop would celebrate the sacraments in the cathedral, but in the parishes priests were appointed to perform liturgical duties: celebrating the Eucharist, baptising, hearing confessions, and other services. In rural areas, many priests continued to hold down a job to support their families, and this was the work they did when not celebrating the sacraments.

Although married priests may originally have been the norm, the model for priesthood and holiness came to be the monks, who began to flourish towards the end of the eighth century. Monks dedicated themselves to lives of holiness, poverty and simplicity. They removed themselves from the material temptations of society and impressed many with their unique witness. Some were ordained as priests and, like Augustine of Canterbury, sent out to evangelise. In the churches they founded they acted as teachers, preachers, and confessors. In monasteries, the monks copied manuscripts of the Bible and other books, and thus these places became centres of learning. St Benedict, the father of Western monasticism, composed the Rule of St Benedict in the middle of the sixth century; and in the later Middle Ages the two great orders of the Dominicans and Franciscans were to be established.

The monastic influence spread to the priests and received tremendous impetus during the time of Pope Gregory VII (*c.* 1021–85), who was himself a monk. Gregory VII stated clearly his idea of papal sovereignty in all the affairs of the Christian community. At this time much of the Church's property and influence was in the hands of wealthy noblemen. They appointed bishops, who would then hand on church property to their own family. In an attempt to restore episcopal allegiance to the Pope, Gregory VII forbade nobles from appointing bishops, declaring such appointments void by papal authority and incurring excommunication for the nobles. He also insisted that bishops abstain from sexual relations and in 1073 made celibacy a condition for entering the order of priests. Gregory VII also declared that priests were not to have other jobs, but were to live on the offerings of the faithful. The reform of the clergy had begun.

Centralisation of authority in Rome increased and the twelfth century saw the appointment of influential bishops to the role of Cardinal, chosen exclusively by the Pope from 1179. Policy was decided and doctrinal orthodoxy upheld through general councils meeting in Rome under the direction of the Pope. A series of councils held at the Lateran Palace between 1123 and 1215 set down many of the markers which still characterise the priesthood today by removing some of the temporal problems that had arisen throughout Europe. Henceforth, lay people could not make church appointments or own church property, and such property or land was not to be hereditary. The First Lateran Council (1123) forbade those in holy orders to marry and ordered all married priests to renounce their wives. The

Second Lateran Council (1139) declared marriages of clerics to be illegal and invalid, and only possible with special dispensation from Rome (and this would require the priest to cease functioning as a priest). By definition, priests were unmarriageable. Married priesthood in the Catholic Church was over.

Changes in the rite of ordination further emphasised the notion that priests belonged to a different order. As well as the laying on of hands, the priest was now vested with the insignia of his office, the vestments to be worn at liturgical ceremonies. This consisted of the stole and chasuble, the latter based on an outdoor cloak worn in Roman times. Other gifts, symbolic of the minister's responsibilities, were also handed over: to the deacon, the Book of the Gospels, to the priest, a chalice and paten, and to the bishop, a ring and crozier.

As theological reflection on ordination developed, it was gradually seen as the only true source of ministry in the Church. This was significant, since it meant that all the other ministries that had flourished in the Church now had a different status. It had been suggested that since many of these ministries were seen as stages on the road to priesthood, then the sacrament of orders was received in small stages. By the end of the twelfth century, however, it was generally held that there was only one sacrament of priesthood, received in several stages.

Ordination, through the power of the bishop, conferred on priests the power to celebrate the Eucharist. Theologians of the twelfth and thirteenth centuries were still troubled, however, by the difference between bishops and priests. In the Eucharist they both mediated between God and humanity. Although both priests and bishops had sacramental powers, only bishops had the authority to confirm and ordain. Power came from God, through the bishop, and he was able to retain certain functions to himself, for he exercised the fullness of priesthood. Priests had the power of priesthood, but it was exercised with the bishop's permission.

Thomas Aquinas further developed the widely-held theological notion of the indelible character applied through ordination. In this sacrament, the ordained received the image of Christ the high priest, the Christ who was perfect victim and perfect priest offering himself on the cross. The life of Christ was one in which he brought God to the world, just as a priest does in the Eucharist. Aquinas believed that ordination transformed the soul, infused it with grace, so that henceforth the priest acted by divine power. As mediators of grace, priests fully received this divine power in ordination, and they exercised it in their sacramental ministry. Priesthood was seen in strictly sacramental terms, directly linked to worship.

REFLECTION

- In the late Middle Ages many bishops were wealthy administrators, whose 'priestly' activity had become secondary or was delegated to priests. How could such a situation develop and what are its dangers?
- The influence of monks meant that holiness was once again associated with priesthood. Can priesthood be reduced to 'doing things', 'being busy', without a life of holiness? How fundamental is holiness to priesthood?
- There seems to be a link between maintaining the Church's ownership of property and celibacy. In the context of what has been termed the 'celibacy debate' how important do you think this is?
- Phrases such as the 'power of ordination' or the 'grace of ordination' are often heard. What do you think is this power and grace? How might such power be exercised?

Protestant reformers and the priesthood

The reform of the Church demanded by the Protestant reformers in the sixteenth century included a change in the notion of priesthood. Luther declared there was no scriptural evidence for the ordained ministry, for the commands to baptise and preach were addressed to the whole Church, not to a special group. Such ministers did exist in the Church, he said, simply for organisational purposes. He strongly believed in the 'priesthood of all believers', but acknowledged that certain people within the community were commissioned to perform certain functions. One of these was the ministry of preaching, whereby the faithful were introduced to the word of God and brought close to him. This ministry, since it nourished faith, was more important than any sacramental ministry. The ministry of the word was to become central to Protestant theology. The background to this lay in the idea that salvation came through conversion; conversion came through listening to God's word; and so it was essential that that word be preached and taught.

Protestants rejected the idea that this sacrament of orders was divinely ordained, conferring some special power. They did not accept the view of authority which suggested that it was passed down from Christ to the Pope, to bishops, and finally to priests. Since many Protestants did not see Eucharist as a sacrifice, the role of the priest was not a cultic one that demanded ritual purity, and so many priests were allowed to marry. Thus, many of the mediaeval notions of priesthood were rejected as the Protestant reformers tried to develop a more pastoral ministry.

The Catholic response in the Council of Trent set a vision of priesthood that remained untouched for more than four hundred years. The document *Doctrine on the Sacrament of Order* placed priesthood in the context of the new sacrifice, that of Christ: the new sacrifice requires a new order of priests, replacing that of the Old Testament. This new order of priests was instituted by Christ, and the Church teaches that 'the power of consecrating, offering and administering His body and blood, and likewise of remitting and retaining sins, was given to the apostles and to their successors in the priesthood'. At Trent the bishops confirmed the existence of minor and major orders through which one eventually became a priest: deacon, subdeacon, acolyte, exorcist, lector, and porter. That order is truly a sacrament conferring grace is deduced from the evidence of Scripture itself: 'That is why I am reminding you now to fan into a flame the gift that God gave you when I laid my hands on you. God's gift was not a spirit of timidity, but the Spirit of power, and love, and self-control' (2 Tim. 1:6–7). The Council's document went on to speak about the indelible character of the sacrament of order and the role and position of bishops, who alone could ordain and confirm.

The Council of Trent had restored an image of priesthood

that was characterised by its sacramental function. Although the statements of the Council might seem limited, it must be remembered that the intention was not to compile a list of the functions of a priest, but to respond to what were viewed as the errors of the reformers. And much of what the Council had to say about priesthood was to be found in documents relating to other sacraments. *The Doctrine on the Sacrament of Matrimony*, for example, prohibited clergy from marrying; elsewhere, bishops were reminded of the fact they were not simply administrators, but had important roles as ministers of the sacraments and of the word.

In many areas the Church was keen for an improved vision of priesthood, and this was typified by the publication in 1563 of a decree on seminaries. Bishops were to see that candidates were suited to ministry and well-trained, thus ensuring a better-educated clergy. Bishops, priests and those training for priesthood were also called to lead exemplary lives, both in terms of their personal morality and daily prayer. One consequence of this focus on priesthood was that priests continued to be the focal point of the life of the local church, where ministry was reserved exclusively for those in orders. That ministry was still largely sacramental, and in subsequent centuries priesthood became very much separated from the world, a ministry responsible purely for holy things. The faithful watched on, as the priests, their link to the divine, administered and celebrated the sacraments for them.

The Second Vatican Council

The model of priesthood set at the the Council of Trent was to last for almost four hundred years. There were two sorts of people in the Church: clergy and laity. Clergy were a distinct class, even superior to lay people; they dedicated themselves to God and passed on the Church's teaching to the laity.

Such a notion was turned on its head at the Second Vatican Council with its emphasis on the Church as the 'People of God',[1] in which ministry stems from baptism: 'The baptised, by regeneration and the anointing of the holy Spirit, are consecrated as a spiritual house and a holy priesthood, that through all their Christian activities they may offer spiritual sacrifices and proclaim the marvels of him who has called them out of darkness into his own wonderful light.'[2] Within the people of God, the 'ministerial priest, by the sacred power that he has, forms and governs the priestly people; in the person of Christ he brings about the Eucharistic sacrifice and offers it to God in the name of all the people'.[3]

Although the traditional teaching on priesthood is the same, the emphasis is much more pastoral than in the past. The Council documents talk about ministers who are at the service of others; priests and deacons are seen as 'helpers', co-workers of the bishops, who should see their priests as sons and friends. The *Decree on the Ministry and Life of Priests* declared:

> . . . it is the first task of priests as co-workers of the bishops to preach the Gospel of God to all . . . The purpose for which priests are consecrated by God through the ministry of the bishop is that they should be made sharers in a special way in Christ's priesthood and, by carrying out sacred functions, act as ministers of him who through his Spirit continually exercises his priestly role for our benefit in the liturgy.[4]

Celebration of the Eucharist, the 'source and the summit of all preaching of the Gospel'[5] is central to the role of the priest. But the priest is not one who simply administers the sacraments. Priests are leaders of the community, counsellors to those in need, men of prayer and humility, who encourage the gifts and talents of lay people.

This increased pastoral emphasis in the Council's vision of priesthood was also reflected in the *Decree on the Training of Priests*, which stated that 'spiritual formation should be closely allied to doctrinal and pastoral training'.[6] The *Decree* went on to say that students for priesthood be:

> . . . especially trained in what is relevant to the sacred ministry, that is, in catechesis and preaching, liturgy and administration of the sacraments, works of charity, meeting the needs of those in error and of unbelievers, and in all

> other pastoral duties. Let them be carefully trained in the art of directing souls, through which all members of the church can be guided towards a fully committed and apostolic Christian life and helped to fulfil the duties of their state.[7]

Even the role of bishops underwent a transformation in the eyes of the Council, which saw them not as rulers but pastors: 'Individual bishops to whose charge particular dioceses are committed, under the authority of the supreme pontiff, care for their flocks in the name of God, as their proper, ordinary and immediate pastors, teaching, sanctifying and governing them.'[8] The image of pastor, of a shepherd caring for his flock, is constantly held up by the Council to express the role of a bishop. By consecration, a bishop became a member of the College of Bishops, with responsibility for the Church throughout the world, and so there is an idea of the communion of all the dioceses being guided by their bishops.

Prior to the Second Vatican Council it was perhaps true to say that clergy were often viewed as being on a pedestal, somewhat remote from people (although it goes without saying that such a generalisation could not be applied to every cleric). In some respects, the Council removed the pedestal. Bishops were no longer seen as remote rulers, but shepherds of the flock. Priesthood was no longer just a matter of saying Mass ('Massing-priests') and upholding the law of the Church, but the clergy were seen as human beings in the service of the word. One of the key elements of priestly training was to become the development of the person, spiritually, emotionally, psychologically. The priest was no longer remote, but was to be involved in the life of the people he served. The whole concept of ministry itself was broadened, with the restoration of the permanent diaconate in 1967, a ministry open to married men, and the call to lay people in general to take on a more active role in the life of the Church.

REFLECTION

- Martin Luther believed the ministry of the word to be the most important ministry, because that excluded no one and was the basic call addressed to all peoples. What do you think of his views? What emphasis is given to the ministry of the word today in Protestant churches and Catholic churches?
- The Council of Trent restored the emphasis on the sacramental role of the priest, but also called for a better-educated and more spiritual clergy. Do you think a priest is characterised by what he does or by what sort of person he is? Is there, can there be a difference?
- Before the Second Vatican Council, the Mass was celebrated by the priest, with his back to the people, and in a language they could not understand but could follow. What image of priesthood do you think this presented?
- Some people today talk about priests no longer being on their pedestals. What do you think this means? In the priests you have encountered, what has struck you most about them and their ministry?

What is *the role of a priest?*

In terms of Holy Orders, the Second Vatican Council was the start of a new type of ministry for priests, a ministry based not simply on liturgical celebrations. Nearly 40 years on from the end of the Council, priests seem to carry out many roles: administering the sacraments, looking after the maintenance of parish buildings, attending meetings of schools, liturgy commissions, finance commissions, pastoral councils, and so on. If this is the case, then what exactly *is* the role of a priest today? Pastors, or administers of the sacraments? Or both? And more?

Priesthood must be seen in the context of service to the people of God, the community of the local church. It is not about power, dictating what can and cannot happen in, for example, the liturgy. Priesthood is one ministry among the many ministries in the Church, with sacramental ministry reserved to the priest. This should be seen not as due simply to some magical, special powers received at ordination, but as linked to what is referred to in the *Rite of Ordination* as the office and dignity of the priest: 'Almighty Father, grant to this servant of yours the dignity of the priesthood. Renew within him the Spirit of holiness. As a co-worker with the order of bishops may he be faithful to the ministry that he receives from you, Lord God, and be to others a model of right conduct.'[9]

The ordained ministry is sharing in the life and mission of the community. The priest is a sign of unity, a symbol of the communion of the people in whose presence and upon whose acclamation he was ordained. The ministerial priesthood serves the common priesthood of all believers. The priest is someone with a special relationship with Christ, in whose name he acts and serves; he has a special relationship to the Church, in whose mission he partakes. He is a sign of Christ and a sign of the Church, someone who cannot be defined simply in terms of what he *does*. Priesthood is perhaps summing up what we saw at the very start of this chapter: a priest is a disciple, an apostle, a presbyter, who presides at the community's celebration of the Eucharist.

REFLECTION

- What do you think is the role of a priest today?
- The *Catechism of the Catholic Church* states that through the ordained ministry 'the presence of Christ as head of the Church is made visible in the midst of the community of believers' (1549). How does the priest make Christ present?
- Priests are called to lead celibate lives as a sign of dedication and service to God. In today's society, what sign can celibacy offer?

A priest should be:
a man who has struggled with God,
a fountain of holiness,
a sinner whom God forgives,

the master of his own desires,
who does not bend in front of the powerful
but who submits himself in front of the poor,
a disciple of the Lord,
head of his flock,
a healer with outstretched arms,
bearer of countless gifts,
a man on the battlefield,
a mother to comfort the sick,
with the wisdom of age
and the trust of childhood,
held out towards heaven, his feet on the ground,
made to be about happiness,
who knows suffering,
who is averse to envy, clairvoyancy,
who expresses himself frankly,
a friend of peace,
enemy of laziness,
always constant . . .
(Written by a priest in the Middle Ages)

9 Matrimony

All Saints is a popular feast day in the Catholic calendar. This Holyday of Obligation on 1 November is when we commemorate all the 'saints' in heaven, those who have not been canonised or have no special feast day of their own. At one of the Masses on All Saints day I remember asking the congregation to think of their favourite saint, to picture that saint. 'The chances are', I said, 'that for most of us the saint we have in mind was not married – because it is actually quite difficult to think of any married saints.' Many of the congregation exchanged knowing glances, as if to say 'Well, if you were married to her/him you'd find it difficult to be a saint!'

Of course, after Mass some people rushed into the sacristy with their list of married saints: Mary, Joseph, the apostles, Margaret Clitherow, Thomas More, to prove that you can be married and be a saint! However it did set me thinking: if married saints are in a minority in the calendar of saints, is that saying something about holiness and marriage?

In all parishes, the sacrament of matrimony presents a number of challenges. Marriages between two Catholics active in the life of the Church are rare; marriages between people of different Christian denominations are the norm, and the level of 'practice of their faith' – however we may define that benchmark – can differ wildly. And yet the demand for 'church weddings' is always there. (Although I have heard recently of weddings at the registry office being followed by photographs in church.)

In recent years the Church of England was split over a suggestion that in one of its documents the phrase 'living in sin' should be replaced by the word 'cohabitation'. Would such a change be interpreted as giving a blessing to what some saw as an improper relationship? A similar interpretation – that cohabitation is approved – was read into suggestions that there should be prayers for a happy engagement. Other ideas included the suggestion that the wedding service should not focus on the ceremony itself but on married life, on the values that a couple should live out in the years to come. As one tabloid newspaper put it, 'Think marriage not weddings say the bishops.'

So what is the sacrament of matrimony about? Is it the wedding day itself, the ceremony, the photos, the video, the reception? Or is there something else?

Marriage

To coin a phrase, 'Marriage is as old as the hills.' It has always been an accepted social custom with many different forms, including both monogamy and polygamy. In every culture marriage has been part of the fabric of society, a basic aspect of how relationships develop. This much is clear from even a simple glance at the opening chapter of the Book of Genesis, written some five hundred years before the time of Jesus: 'God created man in the image of himself, in the image of God he created him, male and female he created them. God blessed them, saying to them, "Be fruitful, multiply, fill the earth and conquer it" ' (Gen. 1:27).

Much of the Old Testament paints a picture of a patriarchal society, with an almost exclusively male domination. Common practice was for a man to have one wife, who was in effect the property of her husband. Contracting a marriage was at the initiative of the man, who usually bought his wife from her father either by working (cf. Jacob) or with money (cf. Gen. 34:11–12, 31:15). The woman was thus inferior and almost servile. The man was the owner of his wife, and adultery (intercourse with a *married* woman) was forbidden on the grounds that it violated property rights. The story of Abraham, Sarah, and Hagar (Gen. 16:2ff.) suggests that a man could have another wife if his first was sterile, or that the wife could give her slave to her husband, with the children being considered her own. Jacob had two wives and each gave him a concubine when they were no longer able to bear children (Gen. 29:15, 30:24), while Esau had three wives (Gen. 26:34, 28:9). Polygamy was motivated by the fertility of the woman, ensuring that the family took precedence. (This explains the practice of a dead man's brother marrying the widow if the man had died without sons – the family must be continued.) Polygamy was also to become a sign of power and riches, with Solomon famous for his 700 wives and 300 concubines!

The Hebrew written law also spoke about divorce, or rather the rejection of the woman by the husband (Deut. 24:1–4). The initiative for divorce is the husband's, the woman cannot reject him. All that is required for divorce is that the husband discovers 'some impropriety' of which to accuse his wife and that he then gives her a 'writ of divorce'. If the woman then marries someone else and is divorced again, the first husband cannot take her back because she has been defiled.

Many of the accepted views on marriage were to change under the prophets, who spoke of the fall of Israel as divine punishment for the immorality of the people. The prophet Hosea spoke of Israel as 'nothing but a whore' for abandoning Yahweh, and yet Yahweh was still faithful, longing to take his people back: 'That is why I am going to lure her and lead her out into the wilderness and speak to her heart . . . There she will respond to me as she did when she was young, as she did when she came out of the land of Egypt' (Hos. 2:15–16). Slowly, the union of man and wife became a symbol and reminder of the love between God and his people. The prophets spoke of the love of God for the people he leads, saves, frees, and waits for their faithful answer. This love is also reflected in the biblical collection of love poems, the Song of Songs, written about 400 BC. The book of Tobit, from the same time, declares the perfect marriage to be that of one man and one woman, and describes the marriage ceremony: Raguel handing over his daughter, Sarah, to Tobias, and giving the couple his blessing, and then Raguel writing out a marriage contract (7:13–14).

Through the message of the prophets, the ideal in marriage had become the faithful love of husband and wife, since this itself was a reflection of the love of God for his chosen people.

Marriage in the New Testament

Jesus may have said relatively little about marriage and divorce, but what he did say was radically new. In Mark's gospel, the Pharisees question Jesus about divorce, mentioning the Old Testament practice of serving a writ of divorce. Jesus' reply was blunt: 'It was because you were so unteachable that he [Moses] wrote this commandment for you. But from the beginning of creation God made them male and female. This is why a man must leave father and mother, and the two become one body. They are no longer two, therefore, but one body. So then, what God has united, man must not divide' (10:5–9); and to the disciples Jesus added, 'The man who divorces his wife and marries another is guilty of adultery against her. And if a woman divorces her husband and marries another she is guilty of adultery too' (10:11–12). A further comment on adultery is to be found in chapter 16 of Luke's gospel, where Jesus says: 'Everyone who divorces his wife and marries another is guilty of adultery, and the man who marries a woman divorced by her husband commits adultery' (16:18).

Jewish practice accepted divorce; but Jesus states that the permanence of marriage stems from the will of God seen in the creation of man and woman, and so divorce is contrary to the will of God. Jesus overrules the Mosaic law, saying that divorce is not part of God's design.

Similar teaching is found in Matthew's gospel, but with a significant addition: 'But I say this to you: everyone who divorces his wife, except for the case of fornication, makes her an adulteress; and anyone who marries a divorced woman commits adultery' (5:32). Is Jesus in fact allowing divorce? Modern Scripture scholars would say that Jesus' original teaching is contained in the passages of Mark and Luke that we have already seen, declaring that divorce is wrong. It is argued that Matthew, writing for Jewish converts, added the phrase 'except for the case of fornication' since it reflects how Jesus' teaching was applied in the Jewish Christian communities some 50 years after Jesus' death and resurrection. Clearly, the early Christian communities were guided by Jesus' teaching that marriage and fidelity were God's will and so could not be altered. In practice, however, divorce was granted for certain reasons.

A fuller picture of early Christian ideas concerning marriage comes from the writings of Paul. He was writing in the belief that the world would end soon, that the second coming of Christ was imminent, and it is in this light that we must take his words that widows and the single should remain as such. Paul reinforces the idea of divorce as unacceptable: 'For the married I have something to say, and this is not from me but from the Lord: a wife must not leave her husband – or if she does leave him, she must either remain unmarried or else make it up with her husband – nor must a husband send his wife away' (1 Cor. 7:10–11). Interestingly, Paul acknowledges the difficulties of marriages between a believer and an unbeliever, and states that if such a marriage does have problems then a divorce can be granted and they will be free to marry again (7:12–16).

The letter to the Ephesians contains an important section on marriage which, some commentators believe, for the first time hints at the sacramental character of marriage.

> Give way to one another in obedience to Christ. Wives should regard their husbands as they regard the Lord, since as Christ is head of the Church and saves the whole body, so is a husband the head of his wife; and as the Church submits to Christ, so should wives to their husbands, in everything. Husbands should love their wives just as Christ loved the Church and sacrificed himself for her to make her holy. He made her clean by washing her in water with a form of words, so that when he took her to himself she would be glorious, with no speck or wrinkle or anything like that, but holy and faultless. In the same way, husbands must love their wives as they love their own bodies; for a man to love his wife is for him to love himself. A man never hates his own body, but he feeds it and looks after it; and that is the way Christ treats the Church, because it is his body – and we are its living parts. For this reason, a man must leave his father and mother and be joined to his wife, and the two will become one body. This mystery has

> many implications; but I am saying it applies to Christ and the Church. To sum up; you too, each one of you, must love his wife as he loves himself; and let every wife respect her husband. (5:21–33)

Using the Middle Ages' technical notion of a sacrament as an outward sign which confers grace, this extract from the letter to the Ephesians seems to hint at some sacramental notion of marriage. It is a symbolic representation of the union of Christ and the Church.

REFLECTION

- What are your memories of wedding days and marriages? What value do you think has been attached to the religious aspect of marriage?
- The world of the Old Testament sometimes saw a wife as the property of her husband. Although this does not mean that they don't love each other, what problems can such an attitude cause?
- The prophets reminded the Israelites of God's unconditional love for them. This was the ideal to follow. What do you think is the link between God's love for his people and marriage?
- The letter to the Ephesians talks of the demanding love expected from husbands and wives. Are there any comments you would make on the extract we have seen?

Marriage in the tradition of the Church

The Scripture passages we have seen would suggest that in the first century the Church, particularly under the influence of Paul's writings, gave a new, religious significance to the social custom of marriage. It raised the status of this social custom and enriched it with a deeper meaning. Origen (*c.* 185–254) assumed that God united two people as one. Christ blessed marriage in a special way and gave it a new dignity. This was shown by his presence at the wedding at Cana and the transformation of the water into wine. Early Church writers said that at Cana Christ blessed marriage, using his divine authority to confer on it a new value.

As yet, however, there was no definitive religious ceremony for marriage. Ignatius of Antioch, writing about the year 110, mentioned the need for the bishop's consent for marriage, but common practice seemed to reflect Roman Law which for marriage simply required the consent of adults. Such a union may have been blessed at the weekly Eucharist celebrated in the Christian community, but this was not common practice. Marriage itself remained an act governed by civil laws, while religious comment was restricted to encouragement for married Christians to live decent lives within the community.

In the fourth century, certain rites, blessings and prayers for marriage begin to appear. Ambrose (*c.* 339–97), Bishop of Milan, talks of a couple being united through the placing of a veil on the woman, the joining of hands, and a blessing; Gregory Nazianzus (329–89) wrote that the right hands of a couple should be united as with the hand of God. The exchange of mutual consent, not the presence of the priest, was considered necessary for a marriage to be valid, and so marriages became family celebrations that took place in a house.

It is perhaps ironic that one of the earliest records of the necessity for marriages to be blessed by a cleric comes from the writings of Pope Siricius (*c.* 334–99), who decreed that the marriages of his clergy had to be blessed by a priest. Gradually, it became common practice for a bishop or priest to give a special blessing to any couple as a sign of approval. This might take place before the wedding feast and might be followed by a celebration of the Eucharist – a forerunner of Nuptial Mass. In time the role of the bishop or priest increased until a complete liturgical ceremony had been developed. It remained only an option, however, and such a ceremony did not become widespread until about the eighth century. By then, the ceremony had been transferred from a house to the church and eventually would only be recognised as valid if conducted in the presence of a priest.

Much of the Church's understanding of marriage was framed in these early centuries by the writings of St Augustine

(354–430). He wrote about the symbolic character of Christian marriage, a sacred sign of the holy bond between Christ and his Church. This was similar to the baptismal character, which remained with the baptised forever. Marriage imprinted on husband and wife the image of the union between Christ and the Church; and like the baptismal character, this could not be received again. It was a seal that could only be broken by the death of husband or wife. Augustine viewed sexual intercourse as sinful, and so one of the benefits of marriage was the fidelity of husband and wife, since marriage discouraged them from seeking sexual pleasure elsewhere. In marriage, sexual intercourse was 'less sinful' if its aim was not pleasure but having children. For Augustine, then, the three 'goods' of marriage were: children, fidelity between husband and wife, and the sacred sign of the union between Christ and the Church. Augustine's is not only the first really consistent teaching on marriage, but it is also the first time there is any hint that marriage might be a sacrament.

As regards divorce and remarriage, there was still no agreed, universal practice. Roman law, which governed marriages, allowed divorce and remarriage. Some bishops in the Church accepted infidelity as grounds for divorce, and allowed men, not women, to remarry. This was presumably due to the text we have already seen in Matthew's gospel: 'But I say this to you: everyone who divorces his wife, except for the case of fornication, makes her an adulteress; and anyone who marries a divorced woman commits adultery' (5:32). In practice, it is unclear as to whether a husband was allowed only to dismiss his wife, or to dismiss her and then remarry. Augustine stated that the innocent party was allowed to send away the adulterer, but was not allowed to remarry.

The Roman Empire was now divided between the East and West, with the Greek part of the Empire based at Byzantium. In the Greek Church, the new code of law promulgated by Emperor Justinian in 542 allowed divorce with remarriage even while the adulterous party was still alive. In the Eastern Churches such a law was accepted without any real problems, and forms part of the Eastern Code of Canon Law to this day.

At the time Justinian's Law came into force in the East, the empire in the West was in a state of chaos and confusion. The 'pagans' who had come into the old Roman Empire had differing practices of divorce and remarriage, and the Church tried to 'christianise' these peoples. Some penitential books dating from the seventh and eighth centuries allow divorce for adultery, but remarriage only for the man. Interesting examples include the Councils of Compiegne and Verberie in France, in 757 and 758, which allowed divorce and remarriage if the other spouse had leprosy, was a slave, or became a monk!

In the ninth century, the Reformation under Charlemagne, the first ruler of the Holy Roman Empire, began. There was a reaction against widespread divorce and a return to the indissolubility of marriage. The Scholastic theologians of the Middle Ages did not discuss the problem, because for them it was never in any doubt. Following Augustine, they saw that Christian marriage is the sign of the union between Christ and his Church, and so must reproduce the image of that union. Christ is always united with his bride, the Church, in a bond that can never be broken.

The variety of practice throughout the Church was due in part to the question as to what ratified a marriage: consent or intercourse? In Rome, a marriage was valid through the couple's consent, not through a blessing by a priest. Some theologians argued that a real marriage did not exist until a couple had had sexual intercourse, while others held that consent made a marriage. The problem was resolved in the twelfth century under Pope Alexander III (d. 1181), who decreed that the basis for a valid marriage was mutual consent. Furthermore, that consent established an unbreakable marriage contract. In this way the Church's traditional teaching on divorce and remarriage was formulated. Alexander III also acknowledged what might be termed the beginnings of annulment, in declaring that church authorities could nullify the marriage if sexual intercourse had not taken place between the couple. Intercourse thus became seen as the action which consummated a marriage contract.

However the Church did not look at marriage in purely legal terms. The decrees of Alexander III were reflected in the theological writings of the time as marriage became more firmly rooted in the sacramental life of the Church. While there was agreement that marriage was one of the seven sacraments, there was some disagreement about how this sacrament conferred grace. One of the major stumbling blocks was over the fact that marriage involved sexual intercourse, which was usually seen as sinful. To counter this, it was stated that a church ceremony in the presence of a priest and with his blessing implied that what happened in marriage was good. More detailed reflection on marriage by many scholastic theologians proposed the idea that the sacred sign in marriage was the consent made by the couple. This was needed for the marriage to be valid, and the marriage contract which it initiated was the sacramental reality of marriage. Since this bond or contract reflected the eternal union between Christ and the Church, it was unbreakable. Marriage could not be dissolved.

The exact nature of the grace associated with the sacrament of marriage had still not been resolved, with some theologians like Bonaventure (*c.* 1217–74) stating that the sacrament conferred not sanctifying grace but 'medicinal grace', which calmed sexual desire and kept it within the limits of fidelity. But with Thomas Aquinas (*c.* 1225–74) came the affirmation that marriage confers a positive and specific grace which does not make marriage different from the other sacraments. The grace of marriage is an aid to holiness in married life and to keeping the vows of marriage in mutual and lasting fidelity. It supports the spiritual unity of husband and wife, that they may love and honour each other as Christ loves the Church. Aquinas, then, believed that Christians were called to the ideal of constant fidelity and perfect love, and that they were given help to strive for this through God's grace in the sacrament of marriage. The sacred sign of this sacrament was not reduced to the giving of consent, but extended to the whole of married life. Marriage was a permanent sacramental sign through which a couple loved and honoured each other and accepted children as God's gift. The greatest expression of love between a man and a woman was the love they expressed in the sacrament of marriage.

One of the final developments of this period came with the writings of the Franciscan Duns Scotus (*c.* 1265–1308), who taught that the minister of the sacrament of marriage was in fact the couple, not the priest. This was the logical conclusion of the process which acknowledged that mutual consent was necessary for a marriage to be valid, and that people validly married received the sacrament. A couple, therefore, administered the sacrament to each other. The role of the priest had become that of a witness.

REFLECTION

- The presence and blessing of a priest was a somewhat late introduction into the marriage ceremony and was interpreted as a sign of approval. Why do you think such an approval was seen as important?
- Augustine spoke of the 'goods' of marriage as children, fidelity between husband and wife, and a sign of the union between Christ and the Church. What comments would you make about these today?
- One of the debates in the Middle Ages was about how a marriage was ratified, by consent or by sexual intercourse. Pope Alexander III decreed that mutual consent was the basis for a marriage. What do you think are the elements or qualities that make up the mutual consent to marry?
- Thomas Aquinas stated that the grace of marriage brings holiness to a married life. In what ways can you see this in married life today?

Onwards from Trent

The Council of Trent was very important in defining the Church's understanding of marriage. Its final session in 1563 was dedicated completely to this sacrament in response to the criticisms of the Protestant reformers.

Martin Luther accepted the importance and holiness of marriage, but he attacked the annulment process and many of the legislative actions of the Catholic Church with regard to marriage. Luther wrote that God had in fact blessed the married state above all others but he denied the sacramental nature of marriage. Nowhere in Scripture did it say that marriage confers grace. Martin Luther felt that it was sufficient to bless a marriage which had been civilly contracted, since marriage was a matter of state jurisdiction. Although personally against divorce, Luther acknowledged it and listed instances where divorce was possible, including adultery and someone abandoning their family.

The response of the Council of Trent was to defend the sacramental nature of marriage and to assert the Church's right to regulate matrimonial matters. The bishops declared that the grace of Christ meant that marriage under the Law of the Gospel was superior to marriage under the old Law and therefore marriage was to be counted among the sacraments. Marriage is indissoluble, sanctifying those who are married and perfecting their natural love. Polygamy was condemned by the bishops, as was the marriage of those in sacred orders.

As for the rite of marriage, the Council of Trent decreed that for a marriage to be valid and sacramental it had to be conducted in the presence of a priest and two witnesses. A public announcement of the intention to marry had to be made at least three weeks prior to the marriage, and after the event all details had to be entered into parish records for the marriage to be canonically legal. This decree resurrected the question about the real minister of the sacrament, for some theologians believed that the real ministers of the sacrament were the couple themselves. But the Council of Trent seemed to imply that the minister of the sacrament was the priest, whose presence was necessary for a marriage to be sacramental.

Melchior Cano (1509–60), a Spanish Dominican, had separated the marriage contract and the sacrament. The former was established through the mutual consent of the couple and could exist validly on its own; the latter came about when the contract was blessed and the marriage thereby became a sacrament. Cano's ideas were well-received and adopted in many countries. At this time nearly all marriages were conducted in church, but the eighteenth and nineteenth centuries saw a rise in civil marriages, with a distinction between the secular aspects of marriage which the state might control and the sacramental aspect which was the domain of the Church. Ironically, Cano's separation of the marriage contract and the sacrament was used by many governments to justify their regulation of civil marriages.

In response, a document issued by Pope Leo XIII in 1880 declared that the marriage contract and the sacrament were inseparable and that there could be no legitimate marriage contract which was not a sacrament. All Christian marriages were valid and sacramental. There is no possible distinction between the contract and the sacrament. For Christians, there is no valid contract if it is not a sacrament. The marriage contract was initiated through mutual consent and that consent also established the marriage as a sacrament. It followed from this that the real ministers of the sacrament were the bride and groom, not the priest.

As to the aims of marriage, the dominant idea was that marriage was still primarily for the procreation and education of children. This did not deny many of the ideas arising in the first half of the twentieth century which emphasised the well-being of the couple as they lived out their commitment to each other. In his 1930 encyclical *Casti Connubii*, Pope Pius XI gave a complete exposition of Catholic teaching on marriage. He reaffirmed the notion that the procreation and education of children was the primary end of marriage, but also stated that the mutual fidelity and commitment of the couple was the 'primary cause and reason of matrimony, so long as marriage is considered, not in its stricter sense as the institution destined for the procreation and education of children, but in the wider sense as a complete and intimate life-partnership and association'.[1] Clearly there was an attempt here to broaden the vision of marriage, to take it beyond what Pope Pius XI called the 'institution' of marriage and introduce a more pastoral and personal dimension.

This was taken even further at the Second Vatican Council, whose *Pastoral Constitution on The Church in the Modern World* devoted a whole chapter to marriage. It defines marriage as an 'intimate partnership of life and love',[2] rooted in the 'contract of its partners, that is, in their irrevocable personal consent'.[3] It is a human act, the mutual giving of two people. The Council avoids using the word 'contract', which seems too legal, using instead the more biblical expression 'covenant', reflecting the covenant between God and the people of Israel.

The Church's teaching on marriage was not altered, but the vision of marriage became less juridical and more personal. The procreation and education of children is still the 'crowning glory' of marriage, the most eloquent expression of married love, but the couple 'help and serve each other by their marriage partnership; they become conscious of their unity and experience it more deeply from day to day'.[4] The sacrament of marriage strengthens a couple, and they are filled 'with the spirit of Christ and their whole life is suffused by faith, hope and charity; thus they increasingly further their own perfection and their mutual sanctification, and together they render glory to God'.[5]

Marriage, then, is a life-giving relationship which reflects the image of God. It is a mutual self-giving which permeates every aspect of married life, and in which children are the supreme gift of marriage.

> Let married people themselves, who are created in the image of the living God and constituted in an authentic personal dignity, be united together in equal affection, agreement of mind and mutual holiness. Thus, in the footsteps of Christ, the principle of life, they will bear witness by their faithful love in the joys and sacrifices of their calling, to that mystery of love which the Lord revealed to the world by his death and resurrection.[6]

The change in emphasis is dramatic and the Council also called for a revision of the rite of marriage reflecting this. The new Rite, allowing a greater choice of readings and prayers, was published in 1969. Marriage was no longer simply juridical, but a personal thing born from the mutual giving of the spouses. The Church's vision of the sacrament of matrimony had shifted from the legal to the personal, a fact reflected also in the Code of Canon Law which defined marriage as 'a covenant, by which a man and a woman establish between themselves a partnership of their whole life, and which of its own very nature is ordered to the well-being of the spouses and to the procreation and upbringing of children'.[7]

Of course it would be wrong to imply that the picture is completely rosy, for separation, divorce and remarriage are common today. The *Catechism of the Catholic Church* acknowledges there 'are some situations where living together becomes practically impossible for a variety of reasons'.[8] The Church allows separation, but does not recognise divorce. Consequently, a new civil union following divorce is not recognised, if the first marriage was valid. While people who are remarried cannot receive communion, the *Catechism* is at pains to point out that the community must be very attentive in making sure such people do not feel ostracised: 'Towards Christians who live in this situation . . . priests and the whole community must manifest an attentive solicitude, so that they do not feel themselves separated from the Church, in whose life they can and must participate as baptised persons.'[9] For some, such carefully chosen words may in fact be little more than that. The pain of divorce and an inability to receive the sacraments may seem a harsh punishment for someone who may have been an 'innocent party'. The question will always be raised as to why second, happier, more stable marriages cannot be recognised. It is perhaps a matter of trying to find the balance between proclaiming that marriage is for life and reflecting the compassion of Jesus, who welcomed those who had failed but who wanted to be in his presence.

REFLECTION

- The Council of Trent stated that for a marriage to be valid and sacramental it had to take place before a priest and two witnesses. Who is the minister of the sacrament and what do you think is the role of those others present?
- Marriage has been described as both a contract and a covenant. What are the merits and disadvantages of these terms? Which do you prefer?
- The shift in emphasis from the legal to the personal has been quite dramatic in its influence on marriage. At any recent marriage you may have attended how has the personal nature of the sacrament come across?

- In what ways do you think the Church can make those who are divorced and remarried still feel part of the community?

'Father, how much will it cost to get married in church?'

Such a question has been asked in parishes up and down the country. In many respects it is a quite natural question, when you think of the actual costs that are often involved in weddings: marriage licences, dresses, receptions, invitations, order of service, flowers, photographers, video production, and so on. Does the question imply that the religious service can be performed for a fixed rate or that it should be thought of in the same terms as the other wedding costs? I would hate to think so.

But many church weddings today do pose a number of pastoral problems. The majority of weddings today are 'mixed marriages', between partners of different Christian denominations. While this in itself is not a problem, the scenario may become more difficult if the couple wishing to have a church wedding do not 'practice' their faith in any recognisable way. A modern-day example could be that of a couple who opt for a special 'Wedding Package Holiday' in, let's say, Barbados. Some months later they would like their child baptised and think it would be quite nice to have their wedding blessed as well, particularly since the Catholic partner is a 'regular' Mass-goer and attends every Christmas. Although that example is extreme, the issues it raises are very real. While there are many couples for whom a church wedding is quite natural because it reflects their belief in the sacrament of marriage and the important role God has in their lives, there are others for whom a church wedding is the 'done' thing, or a ceremony which would be nice for their parents.

The Church's role here is crucial in providing adequate marriage preparation. This is not just a matter of filling in the right forms, but must be a way of helping couples really think about what they are asking from the Church. It is not just a matter of the priest – who is not married – commenting on the importance of marriage. There are many married couples and agencies who help in marriage preparation, so that this important time looks at all aspects of married life. And faith must be at the centre of this. How sad it is if a couple go through a wedding ceremony, celebrating a sacrament they don't really believe in. True Christian marriage is not just a matter of exchanging rights and duties. It is a sacrament whereby the couple reflect the love of Christ for the Church, they make it visible in their own lives, and in this way they form the 'domestic church', the most basic of all Christian communities.

REFLECTION

- What do you think should be included in any 'Marriage Preparation Course'? Who should be giving such a course?
- If you were compiling a list of people to invite to a wedding, would God be on it? What does his presence mean?
- The marriage ceremony itself is full of symbolism, with memorable elements such as the 'giving away' of the bride, the blessing, and the giving of rings. At some weddings the couple light separate candles at the start of the ceremony, and after the blessing and giving of rings they blow out their candles and light a new one together. Were there any such symbolic moments in weddings that you have attended?

It is very consoling to know that this great partnership
into which you are about to enter
is a partnership that was designed by our Creator God
from the very beginning.
At the heart of God's creation is a love story
between a man and a woman.
God formed man and woman to be companions,
partners in a life-long journey of love.
And though that first love story is a love story gone awry,
from that moment on there has existed a wonderful
institution of marriage which is built upon
the partnership of a man and woman in love.

It is that partnership which you seek to form
by standing before God, before the community of the Church
as you promise mutual vows of life-long love and fidelity
to one another
in the sacrament of marriage.

(A marriage homily)[10]

Notes

FOREWORD

[1] *The Teaching of the Catholic Church* (CTS, London, 1985), p.15.

INTRODUCTION

[1] *Catechism of the Catholic Church* (Geoffrey Chapman, London, 1994), 1116.

1 SACRAMENTS – AN OVERVIEW

[1] *A Catechism of Christian Doctrine* (CTS, London, Rev. Ed. 1971).
[2] Herbert McCabe, OP, *The Teaching of the Catholic Church: A New Catechism of Christian Doctrine* (CTS, London, 1985).
[3] *Code of Canon Law*, Canon 840.
[4] Deborah M. Jones, *Focus on Faith* (Kevin Mayhew Publishers, 1987).
[5] Philippe Béguerie and Claude Duchesneau, *How to Understand the Sacraments* (Geoffrey Chapman, London, 1991).
[6] *Catechism of the Catholic Church*, 1131.
[7] Joseph Martos, *Doors to the Sacred – An Historical Introduction to Sacraments in the Catholic Church* (Triumph Books, Liguori, Missouri, 1991), p.29.
[8] *Letters*, 138, 1.
[9] *Sentences*, IV, 1,2.
[10] *Doors to the Sacred*, p.64.
[11] *Summa Theologica* III, question 65, art. 3.
[12] *Decree on the Most Holy Eucharist*, ch. 3.
[13] *The Concise Oxford Dictionary of the Christian Church* (OUP, 1977).
[14] *Decree on the Sacraments*, Canon 1, from J. Neuner, SJ and J. Dupuis, SJ, (eds) *The Christian Faith* (Collins, London, 1983).
[15] *Decree on the Sacraments*, Canon 4.
[16] *Decree on the Sacraments*, Canon 6.
[17] *Decree on the Sacraments*, Canon 9.
[18] *Decree on the Sacraments*, Canon 3.
[19] Taken from *Vatican Council II – Constitutions, Decrees, Declarations*, Austin Flannery, OP (ed.) (Costello Publishing Co. Inc., New York, 1996), n. 62.
[20] *Dogmatic Constitution on the Church*, n. 48.

[21] *Constitution on the Sacred Liturgy,* n. 59.
[22] *Constitution on the Sacred Liturgy,* n. 11.
[23] *Constitution on the Sacred Liturgy,* n. 7.
[24] *Constitution on the Sacred Liturgy,* n. 7.
[25] *Constitution on the Sacred Liturgy,* n. 48.
[26] *Constitution on the Sacred Liturgy,* n. 50.
[27] This was reflected in a pioneering work *Christ, the Sacrament of the Encounter with God* written by the Dutch theologian Edward Schillebeeckx (1963).
[28] *Pastoral Care of the Sick* (Geoffrey Chapman, London, 1983), p.95.
[29] *Catechism of the Catholic Church,* 1069.
[30] *Catechism of the Catholic Church,* 1115.
[31] *Catechism of the Catholic Church,* 1118, 1119.
[32] *Catechism of the Catholic Church,* 1124.
[33] *Catechism of the Catholic Church,* 1127.
[34] *Catechism of the Catholic Church,* 1129.
[35] *Catechism of the Catholic Church,* 1130.
[36] *Catechism of the Catholic Church,* 1140.
[37] *Catechism of the Catholic Church,* 1075.
[38] Tad Guzie, *The Book of Sacramental Basics* (Paulist Press, New York, 1981).

2 THE SACRAMENTS

[1] *Catechism of the Catholic Church,* 1210.
[2] *Catechism of the Catholic Church,* 1211.
[3] *Catechism of the Catholic Church,* 1212.
[4] *Catechism of the Catholic Church,* 1420–21.
[5] *Catechism of the Catholic Church,* 1533–5.

3 BAPTISM

[1] *The Daily Telegraph,* 10 August 1996.
[2] *Guardian,* 30 January 1996.
[3] Cf. *The Apostolic Tradition of Hippolytus,* XXI, 12–18.
[4] *On the Resurrection of the Body,* 8.
[5] *On the Acquisition and Remission of Sins,* 1, 32, 61.
[6] *Decree for the Jacobites,* quoted in *The Christian Faith,* p.392.
[7] *On the Sacraments,* II, 6, 2.
[8] *Large Catechism,* IV, 53.
[9] *Canons on the Sacrament of Baptism* (1547), in *The Christian Faith.*
[10] *Dogmatic Constitution on the Church,* n. 16.
[11] *Constitution on the Sacred Liturgy,* n. 6.
[12] *Constitution on the Sacred Liturgy,* n. 7.
[13] *Dogmatic Constitution on the Church,* n. 7.
[14] *Decree on Ecumenism,* n. 22.
[15] *Decree on Ecumenism,* n. 3.

[16] *Rite of Baptism of Children*, Introduction, n. 4.
[17] Quoted in *Catechism of the Catholic Church*, 1216.

4 CONFIRMATION

[1] By S. Gomez (St Pauls's, 1993).
[2] Ibid., *The Catechist's Guide*, p.4.
[3] *Rite of Confirmation*, n. 42.
[4] Tertullian, *On Baptism*, cc.7, 8.
[5] Council of Elvira, quoted in *The Christian Faith*, p.386.
[6] *The Christian Faith*, p.388.
[7] Ibid., pp.391–2.
[8] *Rite of Confirmation*, n. 42.
[9] *Constitution on the Sacred Liturgy*, n. 71.
[10] *Dogmatic Constitution on the Church*, n. 11.
[11] *Decree on the Apostolate of Lay People*, n. 3.
[12] *Apostolic Constitution.*
[13] *Rite of Confirmation*, Introduction, nn. 7–8.
[14] *Catechism of the Catholic Church*, 1302.
[15] *Catechism of the Catholic Church*, 1303.
[16] *Catechism of the Catholic Church*, 1305.
[17] *Revised Rite of Confirmation*, n. 11.
[18] n. 215.
[19] *Survival Guide to Confirmation – The Catechist's Guide*, pp.4–5.
[20] *Rite of Confirmation*, Introduction, n. 1.
[21] *Rite of Confirmation*, n. 13.
[22] *Code of Canon Law*, Canon 892.
[23] *Catechism of the Catholic Church*, 1311.
[24] In *Communicating Christ to the World*, trans. Thomas S. Lucas, SJ (Sheed and Ward, 1994).

5 EUCHARIST

[1] *The Veritas Pre-Baptism Programme* (Veritas Family Resources, Dublin, 1985).
[2] *Apologia*, ch. 67.
[3] *Doors to the Sacred*, p.214.
[4] *Letter to the Smyrnaeans*, 6.
[5] *Apologia*, ch. 66.
[6] Cf. Pierre Loret, *The Story of the Mass* (Liguori Publications, Missouri, 1982).
[7] *On the Sacraments*, 13–20.
[8] Cf. *The Story of the Mass*, p.47.
[9] *Catechism of the Catholic Church*, 1376.
[10] Cf. *The Christian Faith*, p.408.

[11] *Doctrine on the Most Holy Sacrifice of Mass*, ch. II, taken from *The Christian Faith.*
[12] *Decree on the Most Holy Eucharist*, ch. 1.
[13] *Constitution on the Sacred Liturgy*, n. 1.
[14] *Constitution on the Sacred Liturgy*, n. 14.
[15] *Constitution on the Sacred Liturgy*, n. 48.
[16] *Constitution on the Sacred Liturgy*, n. 10.
[17] *Constitution on the Sacred Liturgy*, n. 47.
[18] *Catechism of the Catholic Church*, 1405.
[19] *Catechism of the Catholic Church*, 1397.
[20] *Constitution on the Sacred Liturgy*, n. 56.
[21] *The Sunday Missal* (Collins, London, 1975).

6 RECONCILATION

[1] *The Christian Faith*, p.453.
[2] *Doctrine on the Sacrament of Penance*, ch. VIII.
[3] *Doctrine on the Sacrament of Penance*, ch. VI.
[4] *Catechism of the Catholic Church*, 1855.
[5] *Catechism of the Catholic Church*, 1862.
[6] *Constitution on the Sacred Liturgy*, n. 72.
[7] *Dogmatic Constitution on the Church*, n. 11.
[8] *Decree on the Ministry and Life of Priests*, n. 5.
[9] *Rite of Penance*, Introduction, n. 10.
[10] *Rite of Penance*, Introduction, n. 1.
[11] *Rite of Penance*, Introduction, n. 5.
[12] *Rite of Penance*, Introduction, n. 6.
[13] *Rite of Penance*, Introduction, n. 8.
[14] *Catechism of the Catholic Church*, 1423–24.

7 ANOINTING OF THE SICK

[1] *The Christian Faith*, p.450.
[2] *Doctrine on the Sacrament of Extreme Unction*, ch. 1.
[3] *Doctrine on the Sacrament of Extreme Unction*, ch. 3.
[4] *Constitution on the Sacred Liturgy*, n. 73.
[5] *Catechism of the Catholic Church*, 1499.
[6] *Catechism of the Catholic Church*, 1505.
[7] *Catechism of the Catholic Church*, 1521.
[8] *Catechism of the Catholic Church*, 1522.
[9] *Pastoral Care of the Sick*, n. 33.
[10] *Pastoral Care of the Sick*, n. 175.
[11] Address at Southwark Cathedral, 28 May 1992.

8 HOLY ORDERS

[1] *Dogmatic Constitution on the Church*, n. 9.
[2] *Dogmatic Constitution on the Church*, n. 10.
[3] *Dogmatic Constitution on the Church*, n. 10.
[4] *Decree on the Ministry and Life of Priests*, nn. 4 and 5.
[5] *Decree on the Ministry and Life of Priests*, n. 5.
[6] *Decree on the Training of Priests*, n. 8.
[7] *Decree on the Training of Priests*, n. 19.
[8] *Decree on the Pastoral Office of Bishops in the Church*, n. 11.
[9] *Rite of Ordination*, n. 22.

9 MATRIMONY

[1] Cf. *The Christian Faith*, p.533
[2] *Pastoral Constitution on the Church in the Modern World*, n. 48.
[3] Ibid.
[4] Ibid.
[5] Ibid.
[6] *Pastoral Constitution on the Church in the Modern World*, n. 52.
[7] *Code of Canon Law*, Canon 1055.
[8] *Catechism of the Catholic Church*, 1649.
[9] *Catechism of the Catholic Church*, 1651.
[10] From *Marriage Homilies*, Liam Swords (ed.) (Fowler Wright Books, 1985).

Bibliography

Bausch, William J., *A New Look at the Sacraments*, The Mercier Press Ltd, Cork, 1983.

Béguerie, Philippe, and **Duchesneau, Claude**, *How To Understand the Sacraments*, SCM Press Ltd, London, 1991.

Bowman, Peg, *At Home with the Sacraments*, Twenty-Third Publications, Mystic, Connecticut, 1991. This is a series of seven short, practical introductions to each of the sacraments.

DeGidio, Sandra, OSM, *Reconciliation: Sacrament With a Future*, St Anthony Messenger Press, Cincinnati, 1985.

Deiss, Lucien, CSSP, *It's The Lord's Supper – The Eucharist of Christians*, Collins, London, 1980.

Falardeau, Ernest, *A Holy and Living Sacrifice – The Eucharist in Christian Perspective*, The Liturgical Press, Collegeville, Minnesota, 1996.

Guzie, Tad, *The Book of Sacramental Basics*, Paulist Press, New York/Mahwah, 1981.

Knight, David, *Confession Can Change Your Life*, St Anthony Messenger Press, Cincinnati, 1984.

Loret, Pierre, C.SS.R., *The Story of the Mass*, Liguori Publications, Missouri, 1982.

McDonald, John F., *The Sacraments in the Christian Life*, St Paul Publications, Slough, England, 1983.

Martos, Joseph, *Doors to the Sacred – A Historical Introduction to Sacraments in the Catholic Church*, Triumph Books/Liguori Publications, Liguori, Missouri, 1991.

Osborne, Kenan B., OFM, *Sacramental Guidelines – A Companion to the New Catechism for Religious Educators*, Paulist Press, New York/Mahwah, 1995.

Osborne, Kenan B., OFM, *Sacramental Theology – A General Introduction*, Paulist Press, New York/Mahwah, 1988.

Taylor, Michael J., SJ (ed.), *The Sacraments – Readings in Contemporary Sacramental Theology*, Alba House, New York, 1981.

Upton, Julia, RSM, *A Church for the Next Generation – Sacraments in Transition*, The Liturgical Press, Collegeville, Minnesota, 1990.

Wilkinson, Peter, *Focus on the Sacraments*, Kevin Mayhew Publishers, Rattlesden, Bury St Edmunds, 1987.